LONGMAN LITERATU

Absent Friends

Alan Ayckbourn

Editor: Jacqueline Fisher

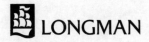

LONGMAN

New Longman Literature
Post-1914 Fiction

Susan Hill **I'm the King of the Castle**   0 582 22173 0
       The Woman in Black   0 582 02660 1
       The Mist in the Mirror   0 582 25399 3
Aldous Huxley   **Brave New World**   0 582 06016 8
Robin Jenks   **The Cone-Gatherers**   0 582 06017 6
Doris Lessing   **The Fifth Child**   0 582 06021 4
Joan Lindsay   **Picnic at Hanging Rock**   0 582 08174 2
Bernard MacLaverty   **Lamb**   0 582 06557 7
Brian Moore   **Lies of Silence**   0 582 08170 X
George Orwell   **Animal Farm**   0 582 06010 9
F Scott Fitzgerald   **The Great Gatsby**   0 582 06023 0
Robert Swindells   **Daz 4 Zoe**   0 582 30243 9
Anne Tyler   **A Slipping-Down Life**   0 582 29247 6
Virginia Woolf   **To the Lighthouse**   0 582 09714 2

Post-1914 Short Stories

Angelou, Goodison, Senior & Walker   **Quartet of Stories**   0 582 28730 8
Stan Barstow   **The Human Element and Other Stories**   0 582 23369 0
Roald Dahl   **A Roald Dahl Selection**   0 582 22281 8
selected by Geoff Barton   **Stories Old and New**   0 582 28931 9
selected by Madhu Bhinda   **Stories from Africa**   0 582 25393 4
       Stories from Asia   0 582 03922 3
selected by Celeste Flower   **Mystery and Horror**   0 582 28928 9
selected by Jane Christopher   **War Stories**   0 582 28927 0
selected by Susan Hill   **Ghost Stories**   0 582 02661 X
selected by Beverley Naidoo,   **Global Tales**   0 582 28929 7
Christine Donovan & Alun Hicks
selected by Andrew Whittle &   **Ten D H Lawrence Short Stories**   0 582 29249 2
Roy Blatchford

Post-1914 Poetry

collected & edited by Roy Blatchford   **Voices of the Great War**   0 582 29248 4
edited by George MacBeth   **Poetry 1900-1975**   0 582 35149 9
edited by Julia Markus & Paul Jordan   **Poems 2**   0 582 25401 9

Post-1914 Plays

Alan Ayckbourn   **Absent Friends**   0 582 30242 0
Terrence Rattigan   **The Winslow Boy**   0 582 06019 2
Jack Rosenthal   **P'Tang, Yang, Kipperbang and other TV Plays**   0 582 22389 X
Willy Russell   **Educating Rita**   0 582 06013 3
       Shirley Valentine   0 582 08173 4
selected by Geoff Barton   **Ten Short Plays**   0 582 25383 7
selected by Michael Marland   **Scenes from Plays**   0 582 25394 2
Peter Shaffer   **The Royal Hunt of the Sun**   0 582 06014 1
       Equus   0 582 09712 6
Bernard Shaw   **Pygmalion**   0 582 06015 X
       Saint Joan   0 582 07786 9
Sheridan, Richard Brinsley   **The Rivals/The School for Scandal**   0 582 25396 9

Contents

INTRODUCTION

The writer on writing

Influences

I inherited a theatre by default, and it was only later I realised I had fallen on my feet. I had this wonderful clear road to a writing career. There was no middle-man telling me it was not suitable.

The Times, 10 April 1996

Imagine, as a playwright, being able to write plays for your own theatre with its own company of actors and having the possibility to direct them in the way you want. It sounds almost too good to be true. Yet, this is exactly the position in which Alan Ayckbourn has found himself.

In April 1996, Ayckbourn's hopes and plans were realised with the opening of the Stephen Joseph Theatre in Scarborough. This was the theatre for which he had campaigned tirelessly since a time some thirty years before when, at the bedside of the dying Joseph, he cut up pieces of card into the shape of the theatre of their dreams.

Stephen Joseph (son of the actress Hermione Gingold and the publisher Michael Joseph), renowned as an anti-establishment theatrical revolutionary, had become Ayckbourn's mentor. He encouraged him to write plays to prevent Ayckbourn as actor complaining about parts given to him within the company:

He had an incredible influence on me but so few people know of him now. Young actors ask me who he was, yet he left this enormous legacy. There are open stages across the country as a result of this extraordinary man in a beanie hat, leather trousers and large boots, who was the scourge of the theatre establishment ... He presented a threat.

The Times, 10 April 1996

When, in 1957, Ayckbourn became a member of Stephen Joseph's Library Theatre Company in Scarborough (on the coast of north-east Yorkshire) 'theatre in the round' was a relatively new concept and was shunned by many theatre-goers and directors for being too 'modern'. Most theatres had more traditional proscenium stages with the audience in front. As Ayckbourn explained in an interview with Michael Coveney, the experiences of working in and writing for this new type of auditorium and theatre company have shaped Ayckbourn's own dramatic thoughts:

> I like small set-ups in the theatre, and Scarborough is still that. Administration can be a bit boring; I really like rehearsing and getting the shows on. Most of my actors stay a long time, which is nice...This strange, quirky way of commissioning my own plays and doing them almost as soon as they're written is a very luxurious way to work. And it seems to be working.
>
> **Plays and Players**, September 1975

Not one to sit in an 'ivory tower' theorising about drama, Ayckbourn – as the Artistic Director of the theatre – is acutely aware of playwriting as a living, breathing entity sometimes sadly stifled through lack of finance:

> It is a performing art and the whole thing starts when the audience arrives and if it doesn't arrive it is no good. You have to take risks occasionally and you may offend. The problem at the moment is that we can't afford to take risks ... Playwriting is an intensely practical craft and the only way you can learn about it is by having your plays put on. In time you know the audience, you know what they will take and, provided it is done right, it's quite extra-ordinary what they will take.
>
> **The Times**, 20 November 1992

The writing process

If you suspend disbelief and picture Alan Ayckbourn starting to write his first play as a gurgling baby on the day he was born you could calculate that he has written roughly one play a year.

Considering, however, Ayckbourn's professional writing began some twenty years later it gives some idea of the speed with which he completes his plays. Almost unbelievably, he explains that writing takes up only ten per cent of his time with the other ninety per cent used for directing and administration. Perhaps one reason for this is that he writes over short condensed periods of time and has driven himself at one point in his life to write two plays in one night: quite a feat for someone who thinks of himself as 'a director who happens to write'.

Somehow the plays keep coming but the process is never as easy as it might appear. In an article by Robert Gore-Langton, the playwright says:

> My nightmare is that because I can't identify their source it will dry up. Every time I finish a play, there is a terrible emptiness for about three weeks and I tell Heather [his partner] I will never write again. Then slowly the ideas start coming back.

> **The Daily Telegraph**, 1 December 1992

Once the process of writing is underway, there can be restrictions and sometimes surprises:

> All I have when I start is the vague idea of a theme and the knowledge of the theatre I'm writing for. I know how many and what kind of actors I've got, so that dictates how many characters I write. I know what, ultimately, the play will say. But within that framework, anything can happen. And frequently does! It was quite on the cards that Diana could have died in the middle of the stage during **Absent Friends**.

> **Plays and Players**, September 1975

Even the characters take time to materialise. Ayckbourn denies basing them on specific people in real life and suggests he meets his characters for the first time as he writes:

> They are blank at first but they talk very fast and by the end they have acquired idiosyncracies. That's it.

> **The Daily Telegraph**, 1 December 1992

Ayckbourn's own experiences, however, have provided some kind of psychological melting pot for the people about whom he writes. The plays deal with marriage, the family and friendship, disillusionment, adultery, moral conscience, destructive rituals, and mental stability. These are serious themes in comedies which often contain dark elements. But where *do* his characters come from?

> I think everyone has important formative years which last until the age of about 16. During that period I was living in Sussex, cruising around with my bank manager stepfather from branch to branch. I lived in those little Sussex towns ... and we used to make regular trips to Brighton. And, at an even earlier time in my life, I lived in <u>real</u> suburbia. Even though I've lived the majority of my life in the north, those people have always remained with me ... one does pick up material which is then translated back into the sort of background one experienced as a child. New material pours in, but it always goes into the filters and comes out in the same sort of setting. I shift around a bit ...

> **Plays and Players**, September 1975

Many of Ayckbourn's plays contain huge emotional traumas which get to the heart of the characters and themes alike:

> I have a faint theory that parenthood is one of the most difficult jobs. Having had children myself at the age of 19, I look back with horror and relief to realise that, thanks to Nature and my wife, they have grown up with a fair proportion of reasonable tendencies. Most people aren't qualified to be parents because they're so busy trying to sort themselves out. Stability is good for children; but then again, perhaps it's good for children to go through the emotions of their parents. I had a stepfather and an ordinary father and, as a result, quite a complicated childhood involving the most traumatic scenes of flying bowls of rice pudding and things. I was probably emotionally starved at the time, but now I rather value the fact that I was subjected to that.

> **Plays and Players**, September 1975

Theatre and life

More and more, Ayckbourn acknowledges his plays to be character-based:

> As I've grown in confidence as a dramatist (confidence, that is, that I can get most of the techniques right most of the time), I have also grown in the conviction that I owe it to the characters I've created to develop and therefore to a certain extent to dictate how a play should run.
>
> I've always had an aversion to comedies that rely upon natty, superimposed dénouements in order to round off the evening. Why comedies should have to do this whereas dramas are allowed to finish as they like is beyond me. As a nation, we show a marked preference for comedy when it comes to playgoing ... At the same time ... one can detect a faint sense of guilt that there is something called enjoyment going on. Should we, people seem to be asking, be sitting here laughing like this? It's to do with the mistaken belief that because it's funny, it can't be serious – which of course isn't true at all. Heavy, no; serious, yes. It would therefore seem unwise to compound this guilt by artificially resolving the play. In other words, it can be funny, but let's make it truthful.
>
> Preface to **Alan Ayckbourn Three Plays**, Penguin 1976

Writing plays containing a range of truthful emotions is just as difficult when writing for children – something with which Ayckbourn has become increasingly preoccupied. His play **Invisible Friends**, written in 1991, is a notable success, but he says writing for children is:

> ...bloody difficult ... Children on the whole don't, I think, want to laugh all the time. I remember howling when Bambi's mother was killed by hunters, and my parents threatening to take me out. 'No,' I said, 'I want to cry. I am enjoying crying.' Kids like a whole palette of emotions. I've recently been throwing them stuff that was fairly adult – sadness, fear, and despair, but not undiluted so that they have nightmares ... I have this touching belief in the possibility that the world might have a happy ending.
>
> **The Daily Telegraph**, 1 December 1992

Getting the balance right is important but Ayckbourn recognises that theatre should reflect life with all its ups and downs:

> It's true that not much of my stuff finishes on an up curve ... On the other hand I hope it doesn't finish dismally desolately – maybe one or two of them do. I once said that a comedy is just a tragedy stopped at a certain point and I think that's true.

The Daily Telegraph, 1 December 1992

Introduction

A life in the theatre

Alan Ayckbourn, one of Britain's most prolific playwrights with some fifty plays to his name, was born on 12 April 1939 in Hampstead, London. His father was Leader of the London Symphony Orchestra and his mother, who later re-married, wrote short stories for women's magazines. At thirteen, he went to Haileybury public school and developed his interest in writing (fostered by his mother) by editing the house magazine and writing plays.

It was a teacher at Haileybury who became the deciding factor in Ayckbourn's career, introducing him at the age of seventeen to his first important theatre contact: the famous, larger-than-life, actor-manager, Sir Donald Wolfit who had his own repertory theatre company. The meeting changed Ayckbourn's life practically overnight and led subsequently to jobs with other companies:

> I had two ambitions. One was to be a journalist, the other to be an actor ... In any school ... there's always one character who is nuts about the theatre. At Haileybury it was the French master, Edgar Matthews, who used to organise amazing productions that we took out on tour during the summer holidays. We toured a Shakespeare to America and Canada for a few weeks ... and this really took on the semblance of a nice-looking life. Mr Matthews used his one big contact, which was Wolfit, and got me a job with him as Assistant Stage Manager ... From there I did the whole basic bit: rep at Worthing, running riot in the scenic and carpentry departments. At Leatherhead I was a more senior Stage Manager and started acting ... Thence to Scarborough, about which I knew nothing ... All I <u>did</u> know about Scarborough was that it was a theatre 'in the round', and that sounded like a good racket as there wouldn't be too much scenery to move about. Stephen

Joseph was running the theatre and ... liked everyone in his theatre to be writing something or other.

Plays and Players, September 1975

From being an actor, stage manager and writer at Scarborough, in 1962 Ayckbourn moved to the Victoria Theatre in Stoke-on-Trent as Associate Director, and then to the BBC in Leeds in 1964 as a radio drama producer during which time he wrote six plays. One of these, **Relatively Speaking**, became his first great commercial success. It is a play in which a man believes the couple he goes to visit are his girlfriend's parents whereas they are in fact his girlfriend's secret lover and the lover's wife!

From Leeds he returned to Scarborough in 1970, eventually becoming Artistic Director, incorporating a two-year sabbatical in 1986 to became a Company Director at the National Theatre in London. There he directed (amongst other plays) a memorable production of Arthur Miller's **A View from the Bridge**, for which he received a Director of the Year award.

Ayckbourn writes at prodigious speed – fifty plays in just over thirty-five years, with five different plays performed in the West End in one year alone. In 1992, he became the Cameron Mackintosh Professor of Contemporary Theatre at St Catherine's College, Oxford, helping writers of all ages. Recently the Writers' Guild of Great Britain honoured him with a Lifetime Achievement Award, and he also received the 1994 Montblanc de la Culture Award for Europe for 'establishing a thriving theatrical tradition in Scarborough and for his dedication and commitment to it'. Scarborough still remains the home for nearly all Ayckbourn's plays before their transfer to London's West End and other theatre venues.

As one of the few playwrights in the country to run a regional theatre, Ayckbourn enthuses about the new permanent theatre building in the town centre which contains two auditoria – the larger of which is in the round. The Stephen Joseph Theatre, Scarborough, will be a monument into the twenty-first century to his theatrical achievements and to the revolutionary Stephen Joseph whose paramount influence Ayckbourn acknowledges with a devoted pride.

Ayckbourn and comedy

The difficult thing about comedy is not what you put in, but what you censor. I've always thought of comedies as tragedies that have been interrupted.

Plays and Players, September 1975

Alan Ayckbourn's comment at the time of the first London production of **Absent Friends**, presents the ultimate puzzle as to just what it is that makes a comedy.

Think about some of the great comic figures of the twentieth-century silent movies era – the deadpan-faced Buster Keaton never smiling; Charlie Chaplin portraying the rather pitiful, underdog tramp; Laurel and Hardy as the incongruous, pathetic pairing. Sometimes the more serious a character or grave a situation, the greater potential there is for comedy.

This is not a new phenomenon in the history of drama:

- In the first scene of Shakespeare's **A Midsummer Night's Dream**, when Egeus demands that his daughter Hermia should marry Demetrius or be put to death or live in a nunnery, it hardly seems an appropriate beginning for comedy;

- Ben Jonson's **Volpone** is a dark comedy about the greed of the main character who receives gifts from the rich citizens of Venice, while they eagerly await what they think will be his imminent death in order to gain his feigned fortune;

- In the French playwright Molière's satirical comedy **Tartuffe**, a hypocrite inveigles his way into a home, attempts to seduce the wife and ruin the family;

- Goldsmith's 1773 play **She Stoops to Conquer**, centres on a misunderstanding, has the character Tony Lumpkin trying to make love to the heroine of the play whom he thinks is a servant, at what he believes is an inn which turns out to be the heroine's father's home!

Why *do* we laugh if someone physically or metaphorically slips on a banana skin? The theatre critic and writer, Michael Billington, uses the term 'light tragedy' rather than 'heavy comedy' for Ayckbourn's plays – plays such as **A Small Family Business** (1987), where characters' morality is compromised by the 'business' of drug-trafficking; **Woman In Mind** (1985), depicting a woman appearing to lose her sanity; **Wildest Dreams** (1991), in which the characters communicate with devastating effect whilst playing a board game in rôle, before the game takes over; or **Man of the Moment** (1988), about a contrived meeting for television between a violent bank robber and his victim years after the crime.

In Ayckbourn's **Absurd Person Singular** (1972), three married couples meet at their respective homes on three consecutive Christmas Eves. In Act Two (set in Eva Jackson's fourth floor flat kitchen), Eva – in a state of manic depression – is trying to commit suicide. She has already contemplated throwing herself out of the window before suffering from vertigo, and has been intercepted trying to run on to the point of a knife. Now alone, she sets about gassing herself in the oven. One of her guests, Jane Hopcroft, obsessed with cleanliness, enters at a crucial moment:

EVA ... *stares at the oven. She goes to it and opens it, looking inside thoughtfully. She reaches inside and removes a casserole dish, opens the lid, wrinkles her nose and carries the dish to the draining-board. Returning to the oven, she removes three shelves and various other odds and ends that seem to have accumulated in there. It is a very dirty oven. She looks at her hands, now grimy, goes to the kitchen drawer and fetches a nearly clean towel. Folding it carefully, she lays it on the floor of the oven. She lies down and sticks her head inside, as if trying it for size. She is apparently dreadfully uncomfortable. She wriggles about to find a satisfactory position.*

The door opens quietly and JANE enters ... JANE carries rather carefully two more glasses she considers dirty. She closes the door. She looks round the kitchen but sees no one. She crosses, rather furtively, to the sink and rinses the glasses. EVA throws an oven tray on to the floor with a clatter. JANE, startled, takes a step back and gives a little squeak. EVA, equally startled, tries to sit up in the oven and hits her head with a clang on the remaining top shelf.

JANE Mrs Jackson, are you all right? You shouldn't be on the cold floor in your condition, you know. You should be in bed. Surely? Here …

She helps EVA to her feet and steers her back to the table.

Now, you sit down here. Don't you worry about that oven now. That oven can wait. You clean it later. No point in damaging your health for an oven, is there? Mind you, I know just what you feel like, though. You suddenly get that urge, don't you? You say, I must clean that oven if it kills me. I shan't sleep, I shan't eat till I've cleaned that oven. It haunts you. I know just that feeling. I'll tell you what I'll do. Never say I'm not a good neighbour – shall I have a go at it for you? How would that be? Would you mind? I mean, it's no trouble for me. I quite enjoy it, actually – and you would do the same for me wouldn't you? Right. That's settled.

Absurd Person Singular

Is this scene comic or tragic?

A careful study of the extract reveals the following theatrical devices, characteristic of Ayckbourn's writing:

- **The running gag**: the audience has seen Eva already fail twice attempting suicide. The repeated action becomes humorous in itself as the audience anticipates how Eva will be prevented from killing herself each time she tries.

- **Character**: characters have been well defined previously so their actions here are truthful and accepted – Jane, with nervous cheerfulness, cannot bear to leave anything dirty whilst Eva, who has been taking pills since a young girl, is silent during this act.

- **Misunderstanding**: here this becomes a **farce**, the elements of which are exaggerated physical action (sometimes repeated);

exaggeration of character; absurd or improbable situations; surprises; unexpected appearances or disclosures.

- **Irony**: this is based on the difference between what is *known* and *thought*. The audience knows Eva is trying to kill herself; Jane does not. This gap between the two is ironic. Jane's punchline: 'You say, I must clean that oven if it kills me' is funny because it is ironic – Jane *thinks* one thing (that Eva is trying to clean the oven) but the audience *knows* the truth (that Eva is trying to gas herself).

- **Language**: the language fits Jane's character. It is full of clichés, repetitions, rhetorical questions (questions not requiring an answer), and is ceaseless.

- **Serious undertones**: the comedy is greater because of the seriousness of Eva's attempted action. Many Ayckbourn plays have extremely bleak, dark sides to them which cause the comic effect to be one of release for the audience.

Absent Friends

Absent Friends was almost a drawing-in of forces. It was significant for me in several ways. Its use of time, for one. The stage action matches real time almost second for second... time span being what it is, had the intended consequence of making the play far more claustrophobic, almost oppressive.

Its single set, its small detailed action, helped. It is a play for a small intimate theatre where one can hear the actors breathing and the silences ticking away. It was a terrifying risk when it was first produced. I'd never pitched anything in quite such a low key before.

Alan Ayckbourn, ***Preface to Alan Ayckbourn***
Three Plays, Penguin 1976

Absent Friends was first performed in June 1974 at the Theatre-in-the-Round at Scarborough, and opened at the Globe Theatre in London in August 1975.

It is a much more intimate play compared with the grand scale and stage innovations of some of his others, such as the trilogy of plays in **The Norman Conquests** (1973), showing simultaneous action in three different places during a weekend; or **Sisterly Feelings** (1979), with a toss of a coin initiating one of two different outcomes at the end of each act; or **A Chorus of Disapproval** (1984) which shows the offstage complexities within a theatre company putting on a play.

The plot in itself is easy to follow: Diana and her husband Paul invite three friends, John and his wife Evelyn, and Marge (her husband Gordon is ill at home) for a Saturday afternoon tea to comfort their old friend Colin whose fiancée has recently drowned. Colin arrives, tea is served and Colin leaves.

There is one set, no mistaken identities, no alternative endings, no unexpected visitors, no aliens. What could possibly go wrong and how can this be a comedy? Within the play's intimacy, however, dark secrets are laid bare, layers concealing the characters' security are stripped away, marriages are scrutinised and the afternoon turns into a disaster. Tensions become unbearable and ultimately funny:

> DIANA ...I think I can speak for all of us, Colin, when I say how very sorry we were to hear about your loss. As I hope you'll realise, we're your friends and – well – and although we didn't know Carol – none of us had the pleasure of meeting her – we feel that in a small way, your grief is our grief. After all, in this world, we are all to some extent – we're all – what's the word...?
>
> PAUL Joined.
>
> DIANA No.
>
> JOHN Related.
>
> MARGE Combined.
>
> DIANA No. Dependent.
>
> PAUL That's what I said.
>
> DIANA No you didn't, you said joined or something.
>
> PAUL It's the same thing. Joined, dependent, means the same.

DIANA   We are all dependent in a way for our own – and, well…no, I'm sorry I've forgotten what I was going to say now. I hope you understand what I meant, anyway.

COLIN   Thank you.

DIANA   *(embarrassed and relieved)* Oh well, that's got that over with, anyway. I mean – more tea, anyone?

MARGE   Give us a chance.

A silence.

Act One, page 36

This extract gives a splendid taster of plot, situation, character, tensions, and use of language combining for great comic effect. Throughout the play, **Absent Friends** has a central irony – a group of people at their nerves' ends trying to comfort an old friend who, quite innocently, seems to create havoc.

Michael Billington, the writer and drama critic sums up as follows:

What is impressive theatrically is the way Ayckbourn builds up an atmosphere of orchestrated chaos. A tea party is meant to be a ritual of decorum and politeness; but before it has got under way and the principal guest has arrived, we have Diana openly accusing Paul of infidelity, Evelyn trying to leave in a huff with her crying baby, Marge on the phone to a desperate Gordon who has spilt cough mixture on his sheet. All these things are happening as Colin is ringing the doorbell trying to get in. All reveal Ayckbourn's familiar ability not merely to <u>tell</u> you things but to <u>show</u> you their consequences.

Macmillan Modern Dramatists: Alan Ayckbourn

Reading log

The 'Study programme' at the back of this book provides many ideas and activities for *after* you have read the play. However, you are likely to give a better response to the text if you make some notes *as* you read. The people who assess your coursework assignments or examination answers are looking for evidence of a personal response to literature; to do well, this should be supported by some close analysis and reference to detail.

Keeping notes as you read should help you to provide this, as well as to keep track of events in the plot, characters and relationships and the time-scheme of the play. When you are reading, stop every so often and use the following prompt questions and suggestions to note down key points and details.

Plot

- What have been the main developments in the plot? Note down exactly where they occur.
- How has the dramatist 'moved the plot on' – for example, by introducing a new character, by a sudden revelation or by a change of setting?
- Is there more than one plot – for example a plot and a sub-plot?
- How do you expect the plot/s to develop? As you read on, consider whether you predicted accurately or whether there have been some surprises.

Characters

- What are your initial impressions of the main character/s? Are these impressions confirmed or altered as you read? How?
- Do any of the main characters change or develop through the play? How and why?
- How are you responding to individual characters? In particular, are you aware that you are identifying or sympathising with one of them? Are you conscious of ways in which the dramatist is making or encouraging you to do this?

Setting

The setting of a play is the place (or places) and time in which the events happen. Sometimes the setting involves a particular community or culture. It can often make an important contribution to the prevailing atmosphere of the work.

- How much detail does the dramatist provide about the setting of the play? How much is this done through production notes and how much through the dialogue?
- As you read, how do you imagine the play would look in performance? Think about the overall design of the production, the set, costumes and lighting.
- Does the setting seem to be just a background against which the action takes place, for example because it is concerned with historical events or with the interrelationship between people and their environment?

Themes

The themes of a work of literature are the *broad* ideas or aspects of experiences which it is about. There are some themes – love, death, war, politics, religion, the environment – which writers have explored throughout the centuries.

- What theme or themes seem to be emerging in the play?
- How is the theme developed? For example, do different characters represent different attitudes or beliefs?
- Does it seem that the writer wants to express his/her attitude to a theme, to raise questions, or just to make the reader reflect on it?

Style

- Is the play written in a naturalistic style – in other words, trying to create the illusion for the audience that it is watching real events? Or does the dramatist use techniques which break or prevent this effect, such as characters speaking directly to the audience in soliloquies or asides, or the use of a chorus?
- Note down any interesting or striking use of language, such as powerful words and images which evoke a sense of atmosphere. Include any recurring or similar images.
- What do you think of the dialogue? Do the 'voices' of the characters sound real and convincing? Make a note of any particular features of the language used in the dialogue, such as dialect, colloquialisms, slang or expletives (swearing).
- Think about the functions of the dialogue in different scenes. For example, is it used to show characters and relationships, to provide dramatic tension, for humour, to explore theme?

Your personal response

- How are your feelings about the play developing as you read? What have you enjoyed or admired most (or least) and why?
- Has the play made you think about or influenced your views on its theme/s?

ABSENT FRIENDS

First produced at the Library Theatre, Scarborough, on 17 June 1974 and subsequently at the Garrick Theatre, London, on 23 July 1975 with the following cast:

PAUL	*Peter Bowles*
DIANA	*Pat Heywood*
JOHN	*Ray Brooks*
EVELYN	*Cheryl Kennedy*
COLIN	*Richard Briers*
MARGE	*Phyllida Law*

The play directed by Eric Thompson
Designed by Derek Cousins

ACT ONE

3 p.m. Saturday.

The open plan living room of a modern executive-style house. Arch-
ways leading off to the kitchen and back doors. Another to the front
door and bedrooms etc. Primarily furnished with English Swedish
style furniture. A lot of wrought iron for gates in lieu of doors and as
used for room dividers. Also artistic frosted glass. Doubtful pictures.
Possibly a bar. It all cost a great deal of money. Parquet floor with
rugs.

At the start, EVELYN, *a heavily made-up, reasonably trendily*
dressed, expressionless girl, is sitting by a pram which she is rocking
absently with one hand whilst gazing blankly out of the window.
Near her, on the table, underneath suitable coverings, tea is laid out
in the form of sandwiches and cakes. Only the teapot and hot water
jug are missing. EVELYN *chews and sings to herself.*

After a moment, DIANA *enters. She is older, mid to later thirties.*
She always gives the impression of being slightly fraught. She smiles
occasionally but it's painful. Her sharp darting eyes don't miss much
after years of suspicions both genuine and unfounded.

DIANA: Have you got him to sleep?

EVELYN: Yes.

DIANA [*looking into the pram*]: Aaah! They look so lovely like
    that. Like little cherubims.

EVELYN [*unenthusiastic*]: Mmm.

DIANA: Just like little cherubims. [*Anxious.*] Should he be
    covered up as much as that, dear?

EVELYN: Yes.

DIANA: Won't he get too hot?

EVELYN: He likes it hot.

DIANA: Oh. I was just worried he wasn't getting enough air.

1

EVELYN: He's all right. He doesn't need much air.

DIANA: Oh, well . . . [*She looks about her.*] Well, I think we're all ready for them. John's on his way, you say?

EVELYN: Yes.

DIANA: How is he these days? I haven't seen John for ages.

EVELYN: He's all right.

DIANA: I haven't seen either of you.

EVELYN: We're all right.

DIANA: Not for ages. Well, I'm glad you could come this afternoon. Colin really will appreciate that, I'm sure. Seeing us all. [*Pause.*]

Paul should be home soon. I think he's playing his squash again.

EVELYN: Oh.

DIANA: Him and his squash. It used to be tennis – now he's squash mad. Squash, squash, squash. Can't see what he sees in it. All afternoon hitting a ball against a wall. It's so noisy. Bang, bang, bang. He's not even out of doors. No fresh air at all. It can't be good for him. Does John play squash?

EVELYN: No.

DIANA: Oh.

EVELYN: He doesn't play anything.

DIANA: Oh, well. He probably doesn't need it. Exercise. Some men don't. My father never took a stroke of exercise. Till he died. He seemed fit enough. He managed to do what he wanted to do. Mind you, he never did very much. He just used to sit and shout at we girls. Most of the time. He got calmer though when he got older. After my mother left him. [*Looking into the pram.*] Did you knit that little jacket for him?

EVELYN: No.

DIANA: Pretty. [*Pause.*] No, there are times when I think that's the principal trouble between Paul and me. I mean, I know now I'm running myself down but Paul basically, he's got much more go – well, I mean let's face it, he's much cleverer than me. Let's face it. Basically. I mean, I was the bright one in our family but I can't keep up with Paul sometimes. When he has one of his moods, I think to myself, now if I was really clever, I could probably talk him round or something but I mean the thing is, really and truly, and I know I'm running myself down when I say this, I don't think I'm really enough for him. He needs me, I can tell that; he doesn't say as much but I know he does. It's just, as I say, I don't think I'm really enough for him. [*She reflects.*] But he couldn't do without me. Make no mistake about that. He's got this amazing energy. I don't know where he finds it. He goes to bed long after me, he's up at dawn, working down here – then off he goes all day... I need my eight hours, it's no good. What I'm saying is really, I wouldn't blame him. Not altogether. If he did. With someone else. You know, another woman. I wouldn't blame him, I wouldn't blame her. Not as long as I was told. Providing I know, that I'm told – all right. Providing I feel able to say to people – 'Yes, I am well aware that my husband is having an affair with such and such or whoever ... it's quite all right. I know all about it. We're both grown-up people, we know what we're doing, he knows I know, she knows I know. So mind your own business.' I'd feel all right about it. But I will not stand deception. I'm simply asking that I be told. Either by him or if not by her. Not necessarily now but sometime. You see.

[*A pause.* EVELYN *is expressionless.*]

I know he is, you see. He's not very clever and he's a very bad liar like most men. If he takes the trouble, like last Saturday, to tell me he's just going down the road to the football match, he might at least choose a day when they're playing at home. [*She lifts the tablecloth and inspects the sandwiches.*] I hope I've made enough tomato. No, I must be told. Otherwise it makes my life impossible. I can't talk to anybody without them ... I expect them, both of them, at least to have some feeling for me. [*She blows her nose.*] Well.

[*The doorbell rings.*]

Excuse me . . .

[DIANA *goes out.*]

[*Offstage dialogue.*]

MARGE: Only me.

DIANA: Marge!

MARGE: I've been shopping, don't laugh.

DIANA: Leave your coat?

MARGE: Oh yes!

[*Sound of shopping bags dropping and laughter.*]

DIANA: How's Gordon?

MARGE: Not too bad . . . [*Bustling in laden with bags.*] . . . poor
little thing – lying there – with his face as white as a sheet . . .

DIANA [*returning*]: Poor thing . . .

MARGE: He looks dreadful . . . Hallo, Evelyn.

EVELYN: Hallo.

MARGE: Oh! Look who's here! Little baby Walter.

EVELYN: Wayne.

MARGE: What?

EVELYN: It's Wayne. His name's Wayne.

DIANA [*laughing*]: Walter . . .

MARGE: I thought it was Walter.

DIANA: Marge, honestly. You can't have a baby called Walter.

MARGE: Well, I don't know. Somebody must have done . . .
[*She screams with laughter. Peering into the pram.*] Oh look.
Look at his skin. It's a lovely skin, Evelyn.

EVELYN: Thank you.

MARGE: Beautiful skin. Hallo, Baby Wayne. Hallo, Wayne.
Google – google – google.

DIANA: Ssh, Marge, she's just got him to sleep.

MARGE [*quieter*]: Diggy diggy diggy. [*Whispering.*] Lovely when
they're asleep.

DIANA: Yes . . .

MARGE [*whispering*]: Looks like his Daddy. Looks like John.

DIANA: You don't have to whisper, Marge. Just don't shout in
his ear.

MARGE [*back to her carriers etc.*]: Look at all this lot. I can't go anywhere.

DIANA: What have you got there?

MARGE: You know what I'm like. You know me . . . oh, guess what I did get?

DIANA: What?

MARGE: Are you ready?

DIANA: Yes.

MARGE: Brace yourself. I got the shoes.

DIANA: You bought them?

MARGE: Just now and I don't care. I passed the shop on the way here. I thought it's no good, I don't care, it's now or never, I'm going to have them, I must have them. So I got them.

DIANA: I must see.

MARGE: Just a minute. Gordon'll go mad . . . [*Rummaging.*] Now, which one did I put them in?

DIANA: It is a shame about Gordon. Gordon's ill, Evelyn, he can't come.

EVELYN: Oh.

MARGE: No. He finally got it. It's been going round and round for months, I knew he'd get it eventually. He was perfectly all right last night, then he woke up this morning and he'd got it. . . [*Finding her shoe bag within another bag.*] Here we are . . . [*Finding something else.*] Oh – nearly forgot. That's for you.

DIANA: For me?

MARGE: It's only a little thing. But I saw one while I was in there and I knew you'd seen mine and wanted one . . .

DIANA: Oh, yes . . .

MARGE [*to* EVELYN]: It's a holder. For those paper towels in the kitchen. Paper towel holder. Have you got one?

EVELYN: No.

MARGE: Remind me, I'll get you one.

DIANA: That's so thoughtful. I must pay you for it.

MARGE: You'll do no such thing.

DIANA: No, Marge, I insist. You're always buying us things.

MARGE: I enjoy it. I like buying presents.

DIANA [*producing her purse*]: How much?

MARGE: I won't take it, put it away.

DIANA: How much was it?

MARGE: Diana, will you put that purse away this minute.

DIANA: No, I'm sorry, Marge, I'm going to pay you.

MARGE: Diana, will you put that away this minute. Evelyn, tell her to put it away . . .

[EVELYN, *during this, has moved to the door and is on the point of going out.*]

DIANA [*noticing her*]: You all right, dear?

EVELYN: Fine.

DIANA: Where are you off to then?

EVELYN: To the lavatory.

DIANA: Oh. I see. Beg your pardon.

[EVELYN *goes out.*]

[*Selecting coins from her purse.*] 20 p. There you are. I don't know how much it was but there you are.

MARGE: Oh, really. [*She leaves the money on the table.*]

DIANA: Am I glad to see you.

MARGE: Why's that?

DIANA: She's been here for ages.

MARGE: Who do you mean – oh, yes. Miss Chatterbox.

DIANA: I know she's been up to something. I don't trust her. I never did.

MARGE: I must show you my shoes. [*Starts to unpack them.*] How do you mean?

DIANA: I know that girl's been up to something.

MARGE: Oh, you mean with . . . ?

DIANA: She and Paul. I know they have.

MARGE: Well . . . [*Producing a pair of very unsuitable shoes.*] There, you see. Aren't they nice?

DIANA: Lovely.

MARGE: They had them in blue which was nicer, actually. But then I had nothing else that would have gone with them.

6

DIANA: He didn't want them to come round here today. That's how I know they're up to something.

MARGE: Who?

DIANA: Evelyn and John. He didn't want them round.

MARGE: Who? Paul didn't?

DIANA: No.

MARGE [*parading around in her shoes*]: Look, you see ... these tights aren't right with them but ...

DIANA: I mean, why should he suddenly not want them round? They've been round here enough in the past and then all of a sudden he doesn't want to see them.

MARGE: Odd. There was another sort, you know, with the strap but I found they cut me across here.

DIANA: They suit you.

MARGE: Yes, I'm very pleased.

DIANA: I tried to get her to say something.

MARGE: Evelyn?

DIANA: Just now.

MARGE: Oh. Did she?

DIANA: No. She's not saying anything. Why should she? I know Paul, you see. I know he's with someone. I'm sure it's her. He came home, went straight upstairs and washed his shirt through the other night. I said, what's got into you? He said, well, what's wrong with me washing my shirt? I said, you've never washed anything in your life. He said, well, we all have to start some time. I said, lovely, but why do you want to start doing it in the middle of the night? And he had no answer to that at all. Nothing. He just stood there with it dripping all over the floor.

MARGE: Well ...

DIANA: After twelve years, you get to know someone.

MARGE: I wonder if these will go with that other coat.

DIANA: What's she doing up there?

MARGE: Well, she's ...

DIANA: I bet she's having a really good snoop around.

MARGE: Oh, Di . . .

DIANA: I bet that's what she's up to. I've never trusted her an inch. She's got one of those really mean little faces, hasn't she?

MARGE: Well . . .

DIANA: I bet it was her that went off with my scarf, you know.

MARGE: I shouldn't think so. Why don't you talk it over with Paul?

DIANA: Paul? We haven't talked for years. Not really. Now he's had his own way and sent the children off to school, there's even less to talk about. I don't know why he wanted them at boarding school. They're neither of them happy. I know they're not. You should see the letters they write.

MARGE: I don't know what to say . . . [*To pram.*] Poogy, poogy. Hallo, Walter.

DIANA: Wayne.

MARGE: Hallo.

DIANA: Don't for God's sake wake him up. He's been bawling his head off half the afternoon. I don't think she feeds him properly.

MARGE: He looks nice and chubby.

DIANA: It doesn't look all there to me.

MARGE: Di!

DIANA: No, truthfully, you look at its eyes.

MARGE: He's asleep.

DIANA: Well, you look at them when it wakes up. Don't tell me that's normal. I mean, our Mark's were never like that. Nor were Julie's. And she's had to wear glasses.

MARGE: She looks lovely in her little glasses.

DIANA: Paul doesn't think so. He won't let her wear them when she's at home.

MARGE: Well, I think he's a lovely baby. I was on at Gordon again the other day about adopting one.

DIANA: What did he say?

MARGE: Still no. He won't hear of it. He's frightened of it, I think. He keeps saying to me, it's not like a dog, Marge. We

8

can't get rid of it if we don't like it and I say, we will like it, we'll grow to like it and then he says, well what happens if we adopt one and then it grows up to be a murderer? Then what do we do? They'll blame us.

DIANA: It's not very likely.

MARGE: Try convincing him. No, he's just going to keep on going with his tests . . . till the cows come home. That reminds me, I must ring him up. I said I would as soon as I got here. See if he's coping. Do you mind?

DIANA: No, go ahead.

MARGE: He's got the phone by his bed.

[MARGE *starts to dial.*]

[EVELYN *returns.*]

DIANA: Find everything?

EVELYN: Fine. [*She checks the baby with a glance, then sits and starts to read a magazine.*]

DIANA: Marge is just phoning her husband.

EVELYN: Oh.

MARGE [*as she stands waiting for an answer, indicating her shoes*]: Do you like these, Evelyn?

EVELYN: Fantastic.

MARGE [*into phone*]: Hallo . . . Jumjums? It's Margie, darling. How are you feeling . . . oh . . . oh. Well listen, Jumjums, can you manage to get across to the chest of drawers, sweetie? . . . by the window, yes . . . you'll find them in the top drawer . . . that's right, darling . . . can you manage that all right on your own . . . right. [*Pause. To them.*] He wants the nose drops, he's all bunged up, poor love . . . [*She stands listening.*]

DIANA [*to* EVELYN]: What are you chewing, dear?

EVELYN: Gum.

DIANA: Oh.

EVELYN: Want a bit?

DIANA: No thanks. We'll be having our tea soon.

MARGE [*into phone*]: Oh, darling . . . you must be careful, Jumjums . . . yes, I know it shouldn't be there . . . never mind, well rub it, rub it better. [*Covering the phone, to the others.*] Banged his leg . . . [*Into phone.*] All right? I'll be here if you want me. You know the number. I'll be home soon . . . yes . . . yes, I will. I'll phone you later. Bye bye, Jumjums, bye bye, darling. Bye. [*Pause.*] Bye bye. [*Pause.*] Bye. [*Rings off.*] Honestly, I don't know what I want children for, living with Gordon. I get through first aid tins like loaves of bread.

DIANA: He's very unlucky, isn't he?

MARGE: Oh, he is. He's so big, you see. I think that's one of his troubles. Being so big. Nothing's really made his size. He bangs his head on buses. He can't sit down in the cinema and he has trouble getting into his trousers. It's a terrible problem. Sixteen stone eight.

DIANA: Yes, that is big.

MARGE: It is, it's very big. His face is small but then he's got quite a small head. It's the rest of him. Somebody the other day said he looked like a polythene bag full of water. [*She laughs.*]

[DIANA *laughs.*]

Oh, dear, you have to laugh.

DIANA: Poor Gordon. It's not fair.

MARGE: He's all right. Bless him. Keeps me out of mischief.

[*They laugh.*]

[*A silence. They look at* EVELYN *who chews on, reading.*]

DIANA [*with a look at* MARGE]: Enjoying that, are you?

EVELYN: It's all right . . .

MARGE: Oh. I've still got these on. [*She starts to change her shoes.*]

DIANA: Be funny seeing Colin again. Three years.

MARGE: I only knew him slightly. He was Gordon's friend really.

DIANA: Yes. It's a pity he'll miss Colin.

MARGE: What exactly happened to this fiancée of his? Did she just die?

DIANA: Drowned.

MARGE: Drowned, oh ...

DIANA: In the sea.

MARGE: Oh.

> [*Throughout the following* MARGE *follows* DIANA's *lips carefully echoing the odd word in agreement.*]

DIANA: We knew him very well, you know. He and Paul were inseparable. And then Colin's job moved him away and he used to write to us occasionally and then he wrote and said he'd met this Carol girl and that they were going to get married – which was a great surprise to us because we always said he'd never let anything get that far and then the next thing we'd heard, she'd drowned. So I said to Paul, we'd better invite him over. I mean, we're still his friends. I doubt if he's got any where he is now because it takes him ages to get to know people and then I thought, well, it might be awkward, embarrassing knowing what to say to him, just Paul and me and since he knew Gordon and you slightly and John – he doesn't know Evelyn of course – I thought it would be nice if we just had a little tea party for him. He'll need his friends.

MARGE: Well, you know me, I'm bound to say the wrong thing so shut me up or I'll put my foot in it. Was she young?

DIANA: Who?

MARGE: His fiancée.

DIANA: Carol? About his age, I think.

MARGE: Oh. Tragic.

DIANA: Yes. [*Aware of* EVELYN *again.*] What are you reading, dear?

EVELYN: Nothing.

DIANA: No, what is it?

EVELYN [*wearily turning back a page and reading flatly*]: Your happiness is keeping that man in your life happy. Twelve tips by a woman psychiatrist.

DIANA: Oh.

MARGE: We can all learn from that.

EVELYN [*reading on remorselessly*]: Tip number one: send him

11

off in the morning with a smile. How many of us first thing just don't bother to make that little extra effort. Have you ever graced the breakfast table without a comb through your hair. Go on, admit it, of course you have. You're only human. Or not done that little extra something to take the shine off your early morning nose. No wonder he escapes behind his paper . . .

DIANA: I must read that.

EVELYN [*unstoppable*]: Go on, live a little and give him the surprise of his life.

DIANA: Yes, that's lovely, Evelyn . . .

EVELYN: Make yourself into his news of the day. You'll live with him till the evening. Tip number two: go on, pamper yourself with a full beauty treatment.

DIANA: Yes, thank you, Evelyn.

EVELYN: What?

DIANA: That's lovely. I'll read it later.

MARGE: We can all learn something from that.

EVELYN: I'm not doing that for my bloody husband. He can stuff it.

[*Pause.*]

MARGE: I'd hate to drown. [*Pause.*] I don't mind anything else. Poison, hanging, shooting – that's never worried me but I'd hate to drown. You look so awful afterwards.

DIANA: Now, we mustn't get morbid. We're here to cheer Colin up when he comes. I know this all happened two months ago now but he's bound to be a bit down. We mustn't let him dwell on it.

MARGE: No. You're quite right.

[*A silence.* PAUL *enters. He has on his track suit bottoms and a sweater. He has obviously been taking exercise.*]

PAUL [*as he comes in*]: Have you seen my shoes anywhere . . .?
[*Breaking off as he sees that they have company.*] Oh, hallo there.

MARGE: Hallo, Paul.

EVELYN [*barely glancing up*]: 'Llo.

PAUL: Mothers' Meeting is it? How are you, Marge?

MARGE: Very well, thank you.

PAUL: How about you, Evelyn?

EVELYN: Eh?

PAUL: Keeping fit?

EVELYN: Yes.

PAUL [*looking into pram*]: What's in here then? Tomorrow's dinner?

EVELYN: No.

PAUL: Oh. I thought it was tomorrow's dinner.

DIANA: Did you have a good game?

PAUL: All right. So so. Not really. Dick didn't turn up. Had to play with this other fellow. Useless. Finished up giving him eight start and playing left-handed. I still beat him. Then he fell over his racquet and broke his glasses so we called it a day. Trouble with that club is, you couldn't improve your game even if you wanted to. No competition. Lot of flabby old men.

EVELYN [*without looking up*]: Hark at Mr Universe.

PAUL: Watch it. [*To* DIANA.] You seen my black shoes?

DIANA: Which ones?

PAUL: The black ones.

DIANA: They're upstairs.

PAUL: Well, they weren't there this morning. How's Gordon?

MARGE: He's not too good today, I'm afraid.

PAUL: Not again.

DIANA: What do you mean, not again?

PAUL: He's always ill. Gordon.

MARGE: Not always.

PAUL: Hasn't been to work for two years, has he?

MARGE: 'Course he has.

DIANA: He's exaggerating.

PAUL: He's a one man casualty ward. Why don't you get him insured, Marge? You'd clean up in a couple of days.

MARGE: Get on . . .

13

PAUL: Right. I'll leave you ladies to it, if you don't mind. Ta ta.
Look after yourselves. I've things to do upstairs

DIANA: Don't be too long, will you, dear?

PAUL: How do you mean?

DIANA: I mean, don't stay up there for too long.

PAUL: No, I've just got a bit of work to do, that's all.

DIANA: Well, tea will be in a minute. You'll be down for that.

PAUL: No. You don't want me down here, I'll –

DIANA: You must come down for tea. Colin's coming.

PAUL: Colin who?

DIANA: Colin. You know, Col –

PAUL: Oh, that Colin. Is he?

DIANA: Oh, don't be stupid. You know he is. I told you.

PAUL: Did you?

DIANA: I arranged it a fortnight ago.

PAUL: You never told me.

DIANA: And I reminded you this morning.

PAUL: You didn't tell me.

DIANA: This morning, I told you.

PAUL: Excuse me, you did not tell me he was coming this
morning. You did not tell me anything this morning. I was
out before you were up.

DIANA: Well, then it must have been yesterday morning.

PAUL: That's more likely. But you still didn't tell me.

DIANA: I told you very distinctly.

MARGE: Perhaps you just forgot, Paul.

PAUL: No. I'm sorry, I didn't forget. I never forget things. You're
talking to the wrong man. I run a business where it's more
than my life's worth to forget things. I've trained myself not
to. I never forget.

MARGE: Well, I'm sorry I . . .

PAUL: Yes, all right. Just don't give me that 'maybe you forgot
bit' because with me it doesn't cut any ice at all . . .

DIANA: Look, Paul, will you stop taking it out on Marge for
some reason . . .

PAUL: I'm not taking it out on anybody. Look, I've got a lot of work to do upstairs . . .

DIANA: Now, Paul, you can't do that. Colin is coming. He is your friend. You can't just go upstairs . . .

PAUL: Excuse me, he is not a friend of mine. He was never a friend of mine . . .

DIANA: How can you say that?

PAUL: I just happened to know him, that's all. You'll just have to say to him when he comes that you're sorry, I had no idea he was coming, nobody told me and that I had a lot of work to do upstairs.

DIANA: You cannot do that . . .

PAUL: I'm sorry . . .

DIANA: You've got no work to do.

PAUL: That's it. No more. I'm not going on with it. I'm going upstairs. I don't want to hear any more about it. I have a lot of work to do. Excuse me, please.

[PAUL *goes out. A silence.*]

DIANA: I told him Colin was coming. I told him over breakfast. While he was eating his cereal. I told him. He always does this. Every time I – [*Tearful.*] I spent ages getting this ready.

MARGE: It's all right, Di . . .

DIANA: It's not all right. He's always doing this. He does it all the time. I told him. Specially . . . [*She hurries out into the kitchen.*]

MARGE: Oh dear.

[EVELYN *gives an amused grunt, ostensibly at her magazine.*]

[MARGE *looks at her.*]

Evelyn, could I have a word with you?

EVELYN: What?

MARGE: I want you to answer me something perfectly honestly. I want you to be absolutely straight with me. Will you do that, please?

EVELYN: What?

MARGE: It's been brought to my notice that you and Paul . . . have . . . well . . .

EVELYN: What?

MARGE: I think you know what I'm talking about.

EVELYN: No.

MARGE: That you and her husband have been . . . is this true? Yes or no?

EVELYN: Is what true?

MARGE: Will you put that magazine down a moment, please.

EVELYN [*laying the magazine aside wearily*]: Well?

MARGE: Is it true or isn't it? Yes or no?

EVELYN: What?

MARGE: Have you been . . . having . . . a love affair with Paul?

EVELYN: No.

MARGE: Truthfully?

EVELYN: I said no.

MARGE: Oh. Well. That's all right then.
    [*Pause.*]

EVELYN: We did it in the back of his car the other afternoon but I wouldn't call that a love affair.

MARGE: You and Paul did?

EVELYN: Yes.

MARGE: How disgusting.

EVELYN: It wasn't very nice.

MARGE: And you have the nerve to come and sit in her house . . .

EVELYN: She asked me. [*Pause.*] She needn't worry. I'm not likely to do it again. He'd just been playing squash, he was horrible.

MARGE: Diana knows about this, you know.

EVELYN: Then he must have told her. I didn't.

MARGE: She's not a fool. She put two and two together. He didn't want you to come here at all this afternoon. That's a sure sign of a guilty conscience.

EVELYN: Most probably because he doesn't like me very much.

MARGE: He liked you enough to . . .

EVELYN: Not after what I said to him.

MARGE: What did you say?

EVELYN: I said thank you very much. That was as exciting as being made love to by a sack of clammy cement and would he kindly drive me home.

MARGE: That wasn't a very nice thing to say.

EVELYN: He's horrible.

MARGE: What a thing to say.

EVELYN: Horrible. Worse than my husband and that's saying a lot.

MARGE: Poor John. God help him being married to you.

EVELYN: Why?

MARGE: Well. Really.

EVELYN: They all think they're experts with women. None of them are usually. And by the time they are, most of them aren't up to it any more.

MARGE: You speak for yourself.

EVELYN: I am. I've tried enough of them to know. [*She reads.*]

MARGE: Your husband will catch up with you one of these days.

EVELYN: He knows.

MARGE: He knows!

EVELYN: Nothing he can do.

MARGE: Does he know about you and Paul?

EVELYN: Probably. He's not going to complain.

MARGE: Why not?

EVELYN: Well – he relies on Paul for business, doesn't he? Without Paul, he's in trouble. Business before pleasure, that's John's motto.

MARGE: Sounds as if it's yours as well.

EVELYN: There's not much pleasure to be had round this place, is there?

MARGE: I'm sorry, I find your attitude quite disgusting. Heartless, cruel and disgusting.

[EVELYN *ignores her and continues her reading.*]

[*At the pram.*] Poor little child. If only he knew. Poor little Walter. Googy, googy . . . You're just a heartless little tart . . . googy, googy.

17

EVELYN: If you're interested, those shoes of yours are a lousy buy.

MARGE: And what would you know about my shoes?

EVELYN: I bought a pair. They split at the sides after two days and the dye comes off on your feet.

MARGE: I've nothing further to say to you.

EVELYN: Anyway, they're out of fashion.

MARGE: I don't wish to listen to you any further.

[*Doorbell. They both wait.*]

One of us had better answer that, hadn't we?

EVELYN: Yes.

[*Doorbell.*]

MARGE: I suppose it had better be me.

[DIANA *enters.*]

DIANA: That was the doorbell, wasn't it?

MARGE: Oh, was it? Yes, we thought we heard it.

DIANA: What if it's Colin? I don't know what I'm going to say if it is ...

[DIANA *goes out.*]

MARGE: You see what you've done.

EVELYN: Beg your pardon?

MARGE: To them. To Paul and her. See the atmosphere between them. All your doing.

EVELYN: Me?

MARGE: Who else?

EVELYN: You really want to know who else?

MARGE: I hope you realize that.

EVELYN: If you really want to know who else, you'd better pass me the phone book. He's halfway through the Yellow Pages by now. If it moves, he's on to it.

[JOHN *enters. A jiggling, restless figure.*]

JOHN: Hallo, hallo.

MARGE: Hallo, John

EVELYN: You took your time.

JOHN: It's only twenty past.

18

EVELYN: You took your time.

JOHN [*amiably*]: Yes. [*He jigs about.*]

MARGE: Where's Di gone to?

JOHN: Dunno. Upstairs, I think. [*Sticking his head into the pram.*] Hallo, son. Say hallo to Daddy.

EVELYN: Don't.

JOHN: Eh?

EVELYN: He's asleep.

JOHN: He shouldn't be. He won't sleep tonight now.

EVELYN: He never does anyway.

JOHN: Keep him awake during the day, that's the secret. Shake his rattle in his ear every ten minutes.

EVELYN: Fantastic.

JOHN: Where's Paul?

MARGE: Upstairs.

JOHN: Oh. Both gone to bed, have they? [*He laughs.*]

[MARGE *glares at* EVELYN.]

No Colin yet?

MARGE: Not yet.

JOHN: Well, I hope he hurries it up. Then we can get it over with.

EVELYN: I thought he was supposed to be a friend of yours.

JOHN: He was, yes.

EVELYN: Sounds like it.

JOHN: I haven't seen him for years. Anyway – I don't know what to say to him. I didn't know this girl of his. I mean, it's difficult.

MARGE: I don't think he'll want to talk about Carol.

JOHN: No?

MARGE: I shouldn't think so. He'll want to forget.

JOHN: I hope so. I hate death. Gives me the creeps.

EVELYN: Get on.

JOHN: It does.

EVELYN: You?

JOHN: I get all . . . uggghhh. [*He shudders.*] Don't talk about it.

19

EVELYN [*laughs*]: Death, death, death.

JOHN: Shut up.

[EVELYN *laughs*.]

[*Silence.* MARGE *takes out her knitting.*]

MARGE: I hope they come down before he arrives.

JOHN: Disgraceful. On a Saturday afternoon. Whatever next. [*Pause. He jigs about some more.*] I got that fuel gauge.

EVELYN: Oh.

JOHN: 90p off it. [*He laughs.*] It had a loose wire. I told the girl it was faulty. She didn't know any better. 90p. [*Pause.*] Got a wing mirror for 30p. Had a screw missing off it. Got one of those round the corner and he let me have some interior carpet for nothing. He was throwing it away. Not a bad day's work, eh?

EVELYN: Great.

JOHN: You're the one who wanted carpet in the car.

EVELYN: Fine.

JOHN: Can't do anything right, can I?

EVELYN: I just know you. It won't fit when you get it in.

JOHN: It'll fit.

EVELYN: No, it won't, because you got it cheap.

JOHN: It'll fit.

EVELYN: Nothing you ever get for us is quite right. I've got a vacuum cleaner with elastic bands holding on the attachments because you got them cheap off another model.

JOHN: Oh, come on.

EVELYN: I've got an electric mixer I can't use because it flings the food halfway up the bloody wall.

JOHN: It's only because it's got the wrong bowl, that's all. Only the bowl's wrong.

EVELYN: Then why haven't we got the right bowl?

JOHN: I'm trying to get hold of one. They're scarce.

EVELYN: But it never did have the right bowl.

JOHN: I know it didn't. How do you think I got it cheap in the first place?

EVELYN: Oh, I give up. [*She reads.*]

JOHN: You're just a trouble-maker, you are. [*He playfully shadow-boxes near her face.*] Bam, bam . . .

EVELYN: Go away.

[JOHN *shadow boxes round the room.*]

[DIANA *returns.*]

JOHN: Here she is. Had a good time up there?

MARGE: Is Paul coming down?

DIANA: I have no idea. I have no idea at all. I have done my best. I have now given up. Most probably it will be left to us. In which case, we'll have to cope with Colin on our own, won't we?

JOHN: Without Paul?

DIANA: Apparently he's far too busy to see his so-called best friend.

JOHN: If Paul's not going to be here, it's going to be a bit . . .

DIANA: Quite. What's that you're knitting, Marge?

MARGE: Oh, just a sweater for Gordon.

DIANA: Lovely colour.

MARGE: Yes, I rather like it. I'm hoping he'll wear it to protect his chest. Once he goes out in that wind . . .

JOHN: How is old Gordon? Is he coming?

MARGE: I'm afraid he's not very well at the moment.

JOHN: Oh, dear. He's had this a long time, hasn't he?

MARGE: Had what?

JOHN: This – er food poisoning, wasn't it?

MARGE: That was weeks ago. This is something quite different.

JOHN: Oh. [*He jigs about.*]

DIANA: Would you like to take a seat, John?

JOHN: No, it's all right, thanks. I don't like sitting down very much.

EVELYN: Sit down, for heaven's sake.

JOHN: I don't like sitting down. I don't enjoy it.

EVELYN: He'll never sit down. I don't think I've ever seen him sit down. He has his meals dancing around the table.

21

JOHN: I prefer standing up, that's all.

[*Pause. He jiggles.*]

DIANA [*tense and shrill*]: John, will you please sit down before you drive me mad.

JOHN [*sitting*]: Sorry. Sorry ...

DIANA: I'm sorry.

JOHN: No, it's me, I'm sorry.

DIANA: I'm sorry, John.

JOHN: No need to be sorry. That's all right.

EVELYN: You'll never get him to sit still, I'll tell you that.

[*They sit.* EVELYN *sings, chews and reads.* JOHN *tries not to fidget.* DIANA *sits, staring ahead of her, steeped in worry.* MARGE *studies her pattern.*]

MARGE [*at length*]: I think I've gone wrong with this. I've got twelve too many stitches. How the dickens did I get twelve too many stitches?

[*At length,* PAUL *enters.*]

JOHN: Hallo, hallo. He's arrived.

[PAUL *stands, surveying the room, making his presence felt. He sits.*]

PAUL: Well. Here I am then.

DIANA: So we see.

PAUL: That's what you wanted, wasn't it?

DIANA: I'm not so sure.

PAUL: Well, make up your mind. I'll go upstairs again.

[*Silence.*]

JOHN: Paul, could we have a quick word about Eastfield, do you think?

PAUL: Not just at the moment, if you don't mind.

JOHN: It's just if I got your okay, I could go ahead with the order.

PAUL: Look, I'm not in the mood to talk about Eastfield just at the moment, John. We're having this riotous tea party. Rude to talk business over tea. [*He discovers the paper towel holder.*] What's this? Where did this come from?

22

DIANA: It's nothing. It's just a holder for the paper towel in the kitchen, that's all.

PAUL: Is it ours?

DIANA: Yes.

PAUL: What have you gone and bought another one for?

DIANA: I didn't.

PAUL: I just put one up the other day. How many of the things do you want?

MARGE: Oh well . . .

PAUL [*laughing to* MARGE]: Kitchen, knee deep in paper towels.

MARGE: It's useful to have a spare.

[*Pause.*]

PAUL: I don't know what we're going to talk to this fellow about, I'm sure. We haven't seen him for three years. I don't even know this girl's name.

DIANA: Carol.

PAUL: Well, that's something. I mean, I can't see what good this is going to do for him. Coming round here talking to us about it.

DIANA: He probably won't want to.

PAUL: Then what else is there to talk about? It's just embarrassing, isn't it?

DIANA: What's embarrassing? Somebody you've known for a long time loses someone very dear to them. Seems natural to ask them round and comfort them a little.

PAUL: Fat lot of comfort he'll get here.

MARGE: We can try. It'll only be for an hour.

JOHN: As long as he doesn't start talking about death, I don't mind. If he starts on about death or dying, I'm off.

EVELYN: I don't know why you came.

JOHN: Well – like Di says, it's – friendly.

EVELYN: You don't like him.

JOHN: Colin? I don't mind him.

EVELYN: You said you didn't like him.

JOHN: I didn't mind him.

PAUL: I didn't like him.

DIANA: You went round with him enough.

PAUL: I did not.

DIANA: You used to come round to our house every Friday and Saturday. You and him. We used to call you the flower pot men.

PAUL: He used to follow me.

DIANA: And Colin always went off with my sister Barbara and I was stuck with you.

PAUL: Very funny.

DIANA: It's true. We both fancied Colin really.

[JOHN *and* MARGE *laugh again.*]

PAUL: That is patently untrue. That is a lie.

DIANA: I was only joking . . .

PAUL: If you want to know what it really was . . .

DIANA: I was joking.

PAUL: If you really want to know . . .

DIANA: It was a joke.

[PAUL *subsides.*]

PAUL: Anyway. Come to that, why do you think we both came round?

DIANA: I don't doubt it.

PAUL: Well.

DIANA: You lost out then, didn't you?

PAUL: So did you.

DIANA: You said it, not me.

MARGE: Look, we really mustn't quarrel.

DIANA: I'm not quarrelling.

PAUL: Neither am I.

MARGE: I mean, Colin's not going to want this. He'll want to feel he's among friends, not enemies.

EVELYN [*in her magazine*]: This is a rotten story in here. This fellow's gone mad just because this girl's kissed him. Running about and singing.

MARGE: I think that's meant to be romantic, Evelyn.

EVELYN: They ought to put him away for good, if you ask me.

DIANA: If you really fancied Barbara, I'm surprised you didn't go off with her. You had the chance.

PAUL: Forget I said it.

DIANA: I mean, why didn't you?

PAUL: Would you all please witness I did not start this conversation?

DIANA: Answer me that.

PAUL: You are all witnesses, thank you.

DIANA: If you fancied her that much . . .

PAUL: Oh, God.

DIANA: Never mind. You're making up for it now, aren't you?

PAUL: What do you mean by that?

MARGE: Now, Di . . .

DIANA: I said, you're making up for it now, aren't you, dearest? With your other little . . .

MARGE: Why don't we all have a cup of tea now? Wouldn't that be a nice idea?

[*The phone starts ringing.*]

PAUL: No. I want that last remark explained if you don't mind.

MARGE: Now, Paul, Paul . . .

DIANA: Never mind.

PAUL: All my other what?

MARGE [*standing between them, arms outstretched*]: Now, Di . . . Paul . . .

DIANA: You know.

JOHN: Should I answer that?

PAUL: All my other what? I want to hear the rest of that sentence.

DIANA: You know perfectly well what I'm talking about.

MARGE: Di . . . Paul . . .

JOHN: I'll answer it, shall I?

PAUL: I have not the slightest idea what you're talking about, I'm sorry.

DIANA [*pointing at* EVELYN]: Well, I'm sure she has. Ask her then.

MARGE: Di . . . Paul . . .

EVELYN: Eh?

JOHN [*who has answered the phone*]: Hallo. Could you speak up please.

DIANA: Yes, you. Don't you sit there looking so innocent and smug. I know all about you.

PAUL: What are you dragging Evelyn into this for?

JOHN: Oh, hallo Gordon. [*To* MARGE.] It's Gordon.

MARGE: Gordon. Oh, my God. [*She snatches the phone from him.*]

DIANA: If anyone has dragged Evelyn into this, it's you.

MARGE: Hallo, Jumjums.

DIANA: You're the one who's dragged her in, literally.

MARGE: My darling, what is it?

PAUL: I don't know what you're talking about. Will somebody kindly tell me what she's talking about?

MARGE: He's spilt his cough mixture in his bed.

DIANA: You know bloody well what I'm talking about. I'm talking about you and her, you bastard.

MARGE: Has it sunk through to the mattress, love?

EVELYN: I'm going home.

DIANA: Yes, you go home, you little bitch.

PAUL: Oh, no you don't. You stay where you are, Evelyn. If she says things like that, she's got to prove them.

DIANA: I don't have to. I know.

EVELYN: Good-bye.

JOHN: We can't go now. Colin's coming.

EVELYN: To hell with him.

PAUL: She's just hysterical.

MARGE: Can you try and sleep on the dry side until I get back?

PAUL: The woman's hysterical. Now listen, Di . . .

DIANA [*screaming*]: Don't come near me.

MARGE: Oh no. Have you got it on your 'jamas as well?

26

[*The baby starts crying.*]

EVELYN [*furious*]: You've woken him up now.

JOHN: I didn't wake him up.

PAUL: I mean, seriously, how can a man live with a woman like
that?

MARGE: Jumjums, how did you get it on your trousers . . . well,
look, take them off, dear. Take the bottoms off.

JOHN: Where are you going?

EVELYN [*starting to push the pram out*]: I'm taking him home.

JOHN: Oh, Evelyn . . .

PAUL: I mean, am I unreasonable?

MARGE: There's some more in the bottom drawer. The stripy
ones.

JOHN [*calling after her*]: Evelyn.

MARGE: Yes, well, you will be sticky. You'll have to wash.
[*Doorbell.*]

DIANA: How you can stand there looking so damned innocent . . .

PAUL: Listen, if you could tell me what I'm being accused of, I
could perhaps answer you.
[*Doorbell.*]

JOHN: I think that's the doorbell.

MARGE: Now, keep warm, Jumjums, keep warm . . .
[EVELYN *re-enters with the pram, baby still crying.*]

JOHN: What are you doing?

EVELYN: I can't get out that way. There's somebody at the
front door.

DIANA: Get out of my house.

EVELYN: I'm trying to.

MARGE: Bye bye, darling.

JOHN: It'll be Colin.

MARGE: Bye.

PAUL: Colin?

EVELYN: I'm taking Wayne in the garden.

MARGE: Bye. [*She hangs up.*]

27

JOHN: Don't go home, Evelyn.

PAUL: Now listen, Di, Marge . . .

EVELYN [*as she goes out*]: I can't, can I?

    [EVELYN *goes out to the kitchen with the pram.*]

MARGE: He has spilt cough mixture not only on the sheet, but on the pillow. . .

    [*Doorbell.*]

PAUL: Would you listen a minute?

MARGE: . . . his clean pyjama bottoms. . .

PAUL: Marge, please. Would you mind? Di, get a grip on yourself, Di.

DIANA: What?

PAUL: Colin is here now at the door.

DIANA: Oh no.

    [DIANA *runs out to the kitchen.*]

PAUL: Di . . .

MARGE: Shall I let him in?

PAUL: Would you mind, Marge. You seem to be the calmest among us.

MARGE: I am not calm, believe me. That linctus will have gone through that undersheet straight into that mattress. [*As she goes.*] I don't know how I'm going to get it out, I don't.

    [JOHN *and* PAUL *are left.*]

    [PAUL *pacing.* JOHN *jiggling.*]

PAUL: Did you tell her?

JOHN: Who?

PAUL: Di.

JOHN: What about?

PAUL: About Evelyn and me.

JOHN: I didn't. Why should I? I mean, as we said, it was just one of those things, wasn't it?

PAUL: Right.

JOHN: Wouldn't happen again.

PAUL: Certainly wouldn't.

JOHN: There you are. We'd settled it, hadn't we?

PAUL: Did Evelyn tell Di?

JOHN: I don't think so.

PAUL: Can't see why she would.

JOHN: No reason at all. Just one of those things, wasn't it? I'm not bitter. It was a bit of a shock when she told me. But I'm not bitter.

PAUL: Somebody told her . . .

[MARGE *ushers in* COLIN.]

MARGE: Here he is.

COLIN: Paul.

PAUL: Colin, my old mate, how are you? [*He embraces him.*]

COLIN: Great to see you, John . . .

JOHN [*shaking his hand*]: Hallo, Col.

COLIN: Oh, it is good to see you both. How are you?

PAUL: Great.

JOHN: Fine.

COLIN: Where are the girls then, where are the girls?

PAUL: Oh – er – Di's just out in the kitchen there.

COLIN: Doing her stuff?

PAUL: Yes, more or less. And – er – Evelyn's with the baby.

COLIN: Hey, yes. You've got a baby.

JOHN: Right.

COLIN: Boy or girl?

JOHN: Boy. Wayne. Four months.

COLIN: Fantastic. That's what you always wanted, didn't you? I always remember that. When the four of us used to get together, you know, you, me, Gordon, Paul – what was it Gordon wanted to be, a cricketer, wasn't it? – you always used to say, I just want to get married and have a son.

JOHN: Right.

COLIN: Fantastic. Congratulations. Sorry to hear about Gordon, Marge. He's ill, you say?

MARGE: I'm afraid so.

COLIN: Poor Gordon, he has all the luck. He wasn't feeling too good when I left, was he? That's right. He was sick at the farewell party.

MARGE: Something he ate.

COLIN [*laughing, to the others*]: Out of me way, out of me way. Do you remember? We were all sitting there, quietly talking and then, out of me way, out of me way. Rushing about the room, everybody scattering for cover. He flings open the door and throws up in the broom cupboard. [*He laughs.*] Nothing serious, I hope?

MARGE: No, no. He always looks worse than he is. [*With a laugh.*] I don't think he's quite at death's door yet.
    [*Pause.*]

COLIN: Good.

MARGE: I'll – see you in a minute.

COLIN: Right.
    [MARGE *goes to the kitchen.*]
    This is all right, this place, isn't it? Very nice indeed. How long have you had this, Paul?

PAUL: Oh, nearly two years.

COLIN: Now we know where the money's going. I'd settle for this. Wouldn't you, John? Yes, I'd settle for this.

JOHN: Yes.

PAUL: You want to sit down?

COLIN: Thanks. [*He sits.*] Very nice.

PAUL: How are you feeling?

COLIN: Oh, pretty fair. Lost a bit of weight lately, that helps.

JOHN: Yes.

PAUL: Col? [*Offers a cigar.*]

COLIN: No thanks.
    [PAUL *takes one, as an afterthought he throws one to* JOHN, *who catches it.*]

JOHN: Thanks, Paul.
    [*Pause.*]

COLIN: What's your wife's name again, John, I forget? Before I meet her.

JOHN: Evelyn.

[JOHN *clicks his lighter intermittently in an effort to make it work.*]

COLIN: Evelyn. That's it. Di did write and tell me. I forgot. Sorry.

JOHN: That's okay. I forget it myself sometimes.

[COLIN *laughs.*]

COLIN: She's not local though, is she?

JOHN: No. She's got relatives.

COLIN: Ah. Will I approve, do you think?

JOHN: Eh?

COLIN: Do you think I'll approve of her?

JOHN: Well, yes. Hope so.

COLIN: She all right, is she, Paul?

PAUL: Eh?

COLIN: This Evelyn of his? Has he done all right for himself, would you say?

PAUL: Oh, yes, he's done all right.

COLIN: John could always pick them.

PAUL: Yes.

[*Pause.*]

[MARGE *enters with mats for the teapot and hot water jug.*]

MARGE [*whispering with embarrassment*]: Excuse me. We're just brewing up. Now, Di wants her handbag a minute. Is it . . . ? Oh yes. Won't be a minute.

[*She goes out.*]

COLIN: She hasn't changed.

PAUL: No.

COLIN: We used to have a name for her, didn't we? When Gordon first took her out.

PAUL: Can't remember.

COLIN: It was . . . can you, John?

JOHN: No. Something. I can't remember.

PAUL: No.

COLIN: It was a beetle or a spider or something. I'll remember, it'll come to me.

[*Pause.*]

JOHN: You're looking well, Col.

COLIN: I feel well.

JOHN: You look it.

[*Pause.*]

COLIN: I'm not early, am I?

PAUL: No, no ...

JOHN: No.

[*Pause.*]

COLIN: Yes. You've certainly done all right for yourself, haven't you, Paul?

PAUL: Now and again.

JOHN: Everything he touches.

COLIN: I bet. You two still fairly thick, I take it?

JOHN: Oh well, you know. When our paths cross. We do each other the odd favour.

PAUL: Generally one way.

JOHN: Oh, come on.

PAUL: Usually.

JOHN: Yes, usually. Not always, but usually.

PAUL: He's still the worst bloody salesman in the country. I'm the only one who'll buy his rotten stuff. I've got about five hundred tins of his rubbish. I can't give it away.

COLIN: What is it?

PAUL: Cat food. So called. That's what they call it. I've never met a cat yet who could eat it and live. Rubbish. I wouldn't give it to a dog.

COLIN: You could try it on Gordon.

JOHN: No, seriously for a moment, Paul, that's what I wanted to talk to you about. That particular line of ours isn't selling so well. It isn't so much content, it's packaging. Now, they have just brought out this new line ...

PAUL: Go on. They've discovered the antidote.

[COLIN *laughs.*]

JOHN: No, seriously, Paul.

PAUL: Not now.

JOHN: No, seriously, one word ...

PAUL: Seriously, John, no.

JOHN: He'll be sorry.

[MARGE *returns.*]

MARGE [*in the same embarrassed whisper, as before*]: Excuse me a minute. Just want to fetch my comb. For Di. Now where did I ...? Oh yes.

[*She finds her own handbag and bends and rummages in it. The men watch her.*]

COLIN: The stick insect.

MARGE [*startled*]: What?

COLIN: Nothing.

[*The men laugh.*]

MARGE [*puzzled, waving the comb*]: We won't be a minute. This is for Di. A comb. For her hair. Excuse me.

[MARGE *goes out.*]

PAUL: Still at the bank, Colin?

COLIN: Yes. Still at the bank.

PAUL: That's what I like to hear.

COLIN: Yes.

[*Pause.*]

PAUL [*rising*]: Look, I think I'll just go and see if I can sort them out out there. Give them a hand. Excuse me.

COLIN: Of course.

PAUL: Won't be a sec.

COLIN: Right.

[PAUL *goes out to kitchen.*]

[JOHN *and* COLIN *rise. They sit. They rise and meet in front of table, laugh. They sit,* COLIN *back in chair,* JOHN *on pouffe. They rise.* COLIN *looks at picture behind bar.*]

COLIN: Great!

JOHN: Terrific!

[COLIN *looks at toy on bar, as* JOHN *leaves for kitchen.* COLIN *turns, sees he is alone, and sits back in chair.*]

[*Everyone returns.* DIANA *with handbag.* PAUL *with teapot followed by* JOHN. MARGE *with hot water jug.* EVELYN *from the garden.*]

DIANA: Hallo, Colin, I'm so sorry.

COLIN: Hallo, Di. [*They kiss.*]

PAUL: Back again.

JOHN [*following* PAUL *round and under the other dialogue.*]: No, the point I'm saying is, that if I were to knock off five per cent and sell the stuff to him for that much less, we could still net a profit of not less than what? – five twenties are a hundred – five eights are forty – less what? – three fives are fifteen – a hundred and twenty five per cent. That's an initial outlay – including transport, of what? – four nines are thirty-six – plus, say, twenty for handling either end – that's fifty-six. Bring it to a round figure – sixty . . .

[PAUL, *throughout this, nods disinterested agreement, his mind on other things. Over this:*]

DIANA: It was so nice you could come. It really was. Now you know Marge, of course, don't you?

COLIN: Yes, yes.

DIANA: Oh, but you don't know Evelyn. This is John's Evelyn.

COLIN: How do you do.

EVELYN: 'Llo.

COLIN: Heard a lot about you.

EVELYN: Oh yes? Who from?

COLIN: Er . . .

DIANA: Sit down, Colin. Let me give you some tea. Sit down, everyone. [*To* JOHN, *who is grinding on to* PAUL.] John dear, do sit down.

JOHN: Oh yes, sorry.

[*Everyone sits.* DIANA *pours tea.*]

COLIN: Do you work at all, Evelyn, or does the baby take up all your time?

EVELYN: No.

COLIN: Ah.

JOHN: She works some days.

COLIN: Oh yes, where's that?

EVELYN: Part-time cashier at the Rollarena.

COLIN: Oh. Is that interesting?

EVELYN: No.

COLIN: Ah.

DIANA: Could you pass these round, Paul? I remembered you liked it strong, Colin.

COLIN: Oh, lovely.

[*Pause.*]

MARGE: Oh! Guess who I saw in the High Street?

DIANA: Who?

MARGE: Mrs Dyson. Grace Dyson.

DIANA: Oh, her.

MARGE: I was surprised. She looked well.

DIANA: Good.

PAUL: Who's Grace Dyson?

MARGE: Oh well, you'd know her as Grace Follett probably.

PAUL: I don't think I know her at all.

JOHN: Remember Ted Walker, Colin?

COLIN: Ted Walker? Oh, Ted Walker, yes. Of course, yes.

JOHN: He's still about.

DIANA: You like yours fairly weak, don't you, Marge?

MARGE: Yes, please. But don't drown it.

[*A silence.*]

COLIN: Do you know what my biggest regret is?

DIANA: What's that, Colin?

COLIN: That none of you ever met Carol.

MARGE: Who?

COLIN: Carol. My ex-fiancée. She was drowned, you know.

35

MARGE: Oh, yes, yes. I know, I know.

COLIN: I wish you'd met her.

DIANA: Yes. [*A pause.*] I think I can speak for all of us, Colin, when I say how very sorry we were to hear about your loss. As I hope you'll realize, we're your friends and – well – and although we didn't know Carol – none of us had the pleasure of meeting her – we feel that in a small way, your grief is our grief. After all, in this world, we are all to some extent – we're all – what's the word . . . ?

PAUL: Joined.

DIANA: No.

JOHN: Related.

MARGE: Combined.

DIANA: No. Dependent.

PAUL: That's what I said.

DIANA: No you didn't, you said joined or something.

PAUL: It's the same thing. Joined, dependent, means the same.

DIANA: We are all dependent in a way for our own – and, well . . . no, I'm sorry I've forgotten what I was going to say now. I hope you understand what I meant, anyway.

COLIN: Thank you.

DIANA [*embarrassed and relieved*]: Oh well, that's got that over with, anyway. I mean – more tea, anyone?

MARGE: Give us a chance.

[*A silence.*]

[COLIN *suddenly slaps his knees and springs to his feet. Everyone jolts.*]

What's the matter?

COLIN: Wait there, wait there.

[COLIN *rushes out to the front door.*]

DIANA [*in a shocked whisper*]: Where's he gone?

PAUL: I don't know.

MARGE: Is he all right?

DIANA: I didn't upset him, did I, saying that?

MARGE: No. Lovely.

JOHN: I'll have a look, shall I?

DIANA: Would you, John. [JOHN exits.]

PAUL: What did you want to get on to that for?

DIANA: What?

PAUL: All that going on about grief and so on.

DIANA: I only said . . .

PAUL: We're supposed to be cheering him up. He didn't want to listen to that.

DIANA: It had to be said.

MARGE: You have to say it.

PAUL: He obviously didn't want to be reminded of it, did he? There was no need to, no need at all. We were all getting along perfectly happily.

DIANA: You can't sit here and not say anything about it.
[JOHN *returns.*]

JOHN: He's gone out the front door.

DIANA: Where to?

JOHN: His car, I think. He's getting something out of the boot.

PAUL: Probably going to hang himself with his tow rope. After what she said.

DIANA: He seemed perfectly recovered. Very cheerful. I thought someone should say something.

PAUL: Cheerful? You can see that was only skin deep.

DIANA: I couldn't.

PAUL: I was talking to him in here. You could tell. He's living on his nerves. On a knife edge. You could tell, couldn't you, John?

JOHN: He seemed quite cheerful.

PAUL: He could snap like that. Any minute. Same with anyone in this situation. Up one minute . . .

JOHN: I've never seen him quite so cheerful.

PAUL: Exactly. All the signs are there. The last thing he wanted to do was to talk about this fiancée of his. It's a known fact, people never . . .

MARGE: Oh yes, they do. My Aunt Angela . . .

PAUL: It is a known fact . . .
[*Slight pause.*]
[*Door bangs.*]

JOHN: He's coming back.

PAUL: Now, not another word about her. Keep it cheerful. For God's sake, Evelyn, try and smile, just for once.
[COLIN *returns. He carries a photo album and an envelope of loose snapshots, all contained, at present, in a large chocolate box.*]

ALL: Ah . . .

COLIN [*breathless*]: Sorry. I forgot to bring these in. It's some photos. You can see what she looked like.

DIANA: Of her?

COLIN: Yes. I thought you'd like to.

MARGE: Oh.

COLIN: Yes. There's one or two quite good ones. Thought you might like to see some. Of course, if you'd rather . . .

PAUL: No, no . . .

COLIN: She was very photogenic. Shall I sit here next to you, Di? Then I can . . . [*He sits next to* DIANA.] Now then. [*Taking snaps from the envelope.*] Ah yes, these are some loose ones I haven't stuck in yet. They're the most recent. Can I give those to you, Marge? I think they're mostly on holiday, those. [*He hands loose snapshots to* MARGE.]

MARGE: Thank you.

COLIN [*with the album*]: These are mostly at home in the garden at her house.

MARGE: Oh, is this her? Oh, she is lovely, Colin. Wasn't she?

DIANA [*as* COLIN *opens the first page*]: Oh.

COLIN: There she is again. That's with her Mum.

DIANA: She's a fine looking woman too.

COLIN: Wonderful. She's been really wonderful. She's got this terrible leg.

DIANA: Ah.

MARGE: Oh, that's a nice one ... Do you want to pass them round, John?

JOHN: Oh yes, sure.

[MARGE *passes them to* JOHN, *who in due course passes them to* PAUL, *who passes them to* EVELYN.]

DIANA: That's nice. Was that her house?

COLIN: No. That's the back of the Natural History Museum, I think.

DIANA: I was going to say ...

COLIN: Went there at Easter.

MARGE [*at photo*]: Oh.

PAUL [*at photo*]: Ah.

DIANA [*at album*]: Oh.

MARGE: Oh look, John, with her little dog, see?

JOHN: Oh yes.

COLIN: That was her mother's.

MARGE: Oh. Sweet little dog.

EVELYN: I like that handbag

COLIN: That's her again. Bit of a saucy one. It's not very good though, the sun's the wrong way.

DIANA: I wish I had a figure like that. It's so nice you brought them, Colin.

MARGE: Oh yes.

DIANA: It's nice, too, that you can look at them without – you know ...

COLIN: Oh no, it doesn't upset me. Not now.

MARGE: That's wonderful.

COLIN: I was upset at the time, you know.

DIANA: Naturally.

COLIN: But – after that – well, it's a funny thing about somebody dying – you never know, till it actually happens, how it's going to affect you, I mean, we all think about death at some time, I suppose, all of us. Either our death, somebody else's

39

death. After all, it's one of the few things we have all got in common ...

[JOHN *has risen and is jiggling about.*]

DIANA: Sit down, John.

[JOHN *sits reluctantly.*]

COLIN: And I suppose when I first met Carol, it must have passed through my mind what would I feel like if I did lose her. And I just couldn't think. I couldn't imagine it. I couldn't imagine my life going on without her. And then it happened. All of a sudden. One afternoon. All over. She was caught in this under-current, there was nothing anybody could do. I wasn't even around. They came and told me. And for about three weeks after that, I couldn't do anything at all. Nothing. I just lay about thinking, remembering and then, all of a sudden, it came to me that if my life ended there and then, by God, I'd have a lot to be grateful for. I mean, first of all, I'd been lucky enough to have known her. I don't know if you've ever met a perfect person. But that's what she was. The only way to describe her. And I, me, I'd had the love of a perfect person. And that's something I can always be grateful for. Even if for nothing else. And then I thought, what the hell am I talking about, my whole life's been like that. All through my childhood, the time I was growing up, all the time I lived here, I've had what a lot of people would probably give their right arm for – friends. Real friends, like John and Paul and Gordon and Di. So, one of the things I just wanted to say, Di – Paul – Marge – John – Evelyn and to Gordon if he was here, is that I'm not bitter about what happened. Because I've been denied my own happiness, I don't envy or begrudge you yours. I just want you to know that, despite everything that happened, in a funny sort of way, I too am very happy.

[*He smiles round at them serenely. A silence. A strange whooping noise. It is* DIANA *starting to weep hysterically. Unable to contain herself, she rushes out. After a moment,* MARGE *fumbles for her handkerchief and blows her nose loudly.* JOHN, *looking sickly, gives* COLIN *a ghastly smile.* PAUL *opens his mouth as if to say something, gives up.* COLIN *stands looking slightly bemused. He looks at* EVELYN. *She looks back at him, expressionless, chewing.*]

COLIN: Did I say the wrong thing?

[EVELYN *shrugs and resumes her reading.*]

CURTAIN

ACT TWO

The same. Time is continuous. 4.15 p.m. All except DIANA.

COLIN [*worriedly*]: I didn't say anything wrong, did I?

PAUL: No, no . . .

JOHN: I think she went to get the . . . [*He can't think of anything.*]

MARGE: You know Di, Colin, she . . .

COLIN: Yes. Sorry.

PAUL: No, no . . .

COLIN: I'll pack these up. I didn't realize . . .

MARGE: No, no . . .

COLIN: Yes. It can be upsetting. I didn't realize . . .

[*He starts to gather up the photos. The others help by passing them to him.*]

I bet I know what the trouble is, Paul.

PAUL: What?

COLIN: Di's been overdoing it again, hasn't she? That was always her trouble. She flings herself into whatever she does. Heart and soul. Remember her with that jumble sale? I've still got this picture of her. Standing there, in the middle of all these old clothes, crying her heart out. Remember that?

PAUL: Yes.

COLIN: I mean, look at this tea. Whoever saw a tea like that?

JOHN: Any chance of a sandwich?

MARGE: Yes, I suppose we'd better . . . [*Holding up a plate of sandwiches.*] John, would you like to pass these round, dear? Here, we've got some plates.

[JOHN *rises.*]

PAUL [*also rising*]: It's all right. I'll . . .

COLIN [*who has gathered in all his photos*]: Is that the lot?

42

MARGE [*handing* PAUL *sideplates with paper napkins*]: Here you are. [*To* COLIN.] We'd all love to have another look at them later.

JOHN [*passing round the sandwiches, muttering*]: Great.

COLIN: Yes, well, possibly. I hope Di's all right.

PAUL: Oh, yes . . .

MARGE: Oh, yes. She'll be fine. Fine. She's very sensitive.

COLIN: Oh, yes. I think that's what makes her a wonderful person, you know.

MARGE: Yes, yes. I think we could all learn from her example. She's so loyal and trusting . . .

COLIN: Yes. She's got a lot of the qualities Carol had in that respect. You're a lucky man, Paul.

PAUL: Yes.

COLIN [*laughing suddenly*]: It could have been me at one point, couldn't it? Remember? Diana and me instead of Diana and you.

PAUL: Could it?

COLIN: Oh, come on, you haven't forgotten that. [*To the others.*] We were both after her – him and me – at one time.

MARGE: Were you really?

COLIN: Oh, yes. And I think it's fair to say, isn't it, Paul, fair to say, that there was one moment in time when I don't think she could honestly choose between us.

MARGE: Really, I didn't know.

COLIN: Still, it all ended happily, didn't it? Lucky old Paul, and if I'd married Di, I wouldn't have met Carol . . .

MARGE: Yes.

[*Pause.*]

COLIN: Talking of Carol, it's an odd thing you know. I'm sure this is fairly common. I mean, you read about it happening but there are times when I feel that she's still around somewhere. Some part of her. Her spirit or whatever you call it. She could be in this room at this moment. Odd, isn't it?

MARGE: It does happen to people. My Aunt Angela –

COLIN: I mean, I know for certain in my mind that she's dead. There's no doubt that she's dead. I saw her lying there dead with my own eyes ...

[JOHN *rises and jiggles about.*]

But nevertheless, as I say, I feel that here, around here somewhere, she's watching us. She can't communicate but she's watching me. Taking care of me.

JOHN [*moving to the door*]: Excuse me.

MARGE: All right, John?

JOHN: Yes, I'm just going to see if – Di's all right ...

[JOHN *goes out to the kitchen.*]

COLIN: Good old John. He still can't sit still, can he?

MARGE: No.

COLIN: You took on a real live wire there, Evelyn.

EVELYN: Oh yes?

COLIN: How do you manage to keep up with him?

EVELYN: I don't bother.

COLIN: You'll have to get up early in the morning to catch John.

EVELYN: I do. Every morning. He doesn't wake up at all unless I wake him.

COLIN: Oh well, that's marriage.

EVELYN: How do you know?

COLIN: Well, I mean ...

MARGE: Evelyn ...

EVELYN: What?

MARGE: Don't be so ...

EVELYN: What?

MARGE: Never mind.

PAUL: How long had you known Carol, Colin?

COLIN: Just over a year. Fourteen months, twenty-three days.

PAUL: Ah well. Time would have told.

COLIN: Told what?

PAUL: I mean, well – I mean, to be fair you hadn't time really to get to know her. Not really.

COLIN: I think I knew Carol better than I've ever known anybody before or since, Paul.

PAUL: Oh. Well. I'm sure . . .

[DIANA *returns with a jug of cream.*]

DIANA: I'm so sorry, everyone. I just wanted to make sure I'd turned the gas off. Now this is the cream for the trifle afterwards if anybody wants any. I've left that out there in the cool till we've cleared away some of this. Oh good, you've started the sandwiches.

MARGE: Yes, I hope you didn't . . .

DIANA: No, no. They're there to be eaten.

COLIN: I'm very sorry, Di, if I upset you with – what I said . . .

DIANA: Oh no, Colin, no. Not at all. John's outside checking on the baby, Evelyn.

EVELYN: Oh.

DIANA: He thought one of you should. He's wonderful with that baby, Colin. You should see him.

COLIN: I bet.

DIANA: Does all the things a mother should and better.

[EVELYN *clicks her tongue. She picks up the magazine and buries her nose in it rudely.*]

COLIN: You all right, Evelyn?

EVELYN: Eh?

COLIN: Anything the matter? You seem a bit down.

EVELYN: No. No. No . . .

MARGE: It's just her manner.

DIANA: You get used to it eventually.

COLIN: Oh. Do you know something, Evelyn? Now I'm talking off the top of my head now because I've only just met you, I don't really know you – but – I think Paul will back me on this, won't you, Paul – I've always had this knack – gift if you like, I suppose you could call it – for being able to sum people up pretty quickly. Sometimes I've just got to meet them, exchange a few words with them and on occasions, not always

45

but on occasions, I know more about that particular person than they know about themselves. Now I could be wrong, as I say this is straight off the top but I would say just from the brief time I've had to study you, I would say something's bothering you. Right or wrong?

EVELYN: Right.

COLIN: There you are. Now, I'm going to go a bit further and I warn you I'm going to stick my neck right out now and say one of your worries is John. Right?

EVELYN: Amazing.

COLIN: No, not altogether. You see, I think I know what it is – [*to the others.*] excuse me, I'm just putting Evelyn straight – right. Number one. John is a very high powered individual – can't sit still, always on the move. We all know him in this room very well. Probably better than you do, Evelyn. You see, we've known him for years. He's an extrovert, good brain, clever – wonderful with his hands. The sort of fellow, if you're in trouble, it's John you go to. John is number one. Never let you down. The bee's knees. But – and there's a big but – and I think everyone here will agree with this – Marge, Di, Paul, Gordon if he was here – what we, every one of us, have always said about John is – God help the woman he marries. Because every day of their lives together, she is going to have to get used to the fact that John is going to be the driver while she is going to have to spend most of her life in the back seat.

[*He pauses for effect and gets one.*]

So. My advice is, don't let your personality – because I can see there's a lovely personality hiding under there – don't let that get buried away. Because he won't thank you for it in the end. Nobody will. Get in the habit of giving yourself to people, if you know what I mean, and you'll get a lot more back, believe me. I'm a giver. It's natural, how I was born, nothing virtuous about it, per se – just the way I'm made. Others have to work at it. Carol was another giver. She'd give you everything. Everything she had.

[*Silence.*]

MARGE: True. True . . .

COLIN: Sorry. I'm preaching. I can feel it. Sorry, Evelyn. Beg your pardon. I just happen to be an expert on John, that's all. I'm an expert on Paul here as well. Shall I tell you about Paul?

EVELYN: No thanks.

COLIN: No. Better not. He gets embarrassed.

DIANA: Yes. Another sandwich, everyone?

COLIN: Oh, ta.

[JOHN *returns from the garden.*]

MARGE: Is he all right?

JOHN: Yes. Fast asleep now.

COLIN: Just been talking about you.

JOHN: Who has?

EVELYN: Him, mainly.

COLIN: Me, mainly.

JOHN: Oh.

MARGE: Yes, now we know, don't we, everyone?

EVELYN: We certainly do.

[*Pause. Sandwiches are passed. Everyone settles.*]

COLIN: Memory test. Do you remember, does anyone remember, the last time we were all together like this? I mean as a group. If you count Gordon and don't count Evelyn. Does anyone remember?

DIANA: No. When would that have been?

PAUL: Dick's anniversary.

COLIN: No, no. Months after that.

MARGE: I give up.

COLIN: Do the words Stately Home remind you of anything?

DIANA: Stately Home? You mean that place?

JOHN: That place, yes . . .

PAUL: Oh, grief . . .

MARGE: The one day of the year we chose . . .

DIANA: And it's closed.

47

MARGE: That was dreadful, wasn't it?

PAUL: Proper waste of petrol.

DIANA: And then the rain.

MARGE: All that rain.

DIANA: And that was the day I lost that glove.

MARGE: Yes. That's it. And then Gordon lost the convoy. We were driving up here, down there, trying to find you.

JOHN: It was all right for you. We were sitting in that lay-by for two hours while you were seeing the countryside.

COLIN: Yes, but it was a marvellous day, wasn't it?

JOHN: Was it?

COLIN: Oh, it was a great laugh – sorry, Evelyn, this must be very boring for you, love –

EVELYN: Yes.

COLIN: Remember that fabulous picnic?

DIANA: All I remember is running from one car to the other in the rain with the thermos flask.

COLIN: And we found a great place for tea.

PAUL: Where they overcharged us.

COLIN: It was great. I'll always remember that.

JOHN: Yes.

COLIN: What a marvellous day that was.

DIANA [doubtfully]: Yes.

MARGE: I suppose so, yes.

COLIN: You missed something there, Evelyn.

EVELYN: Sounds like it.

[Pause.]

COLIN: Poor old Gordon. Lying in bed while we're scoffing ourselves.

MARGE: Yes, shame.

COLIN: Now, Gordon's the opposite to John, isn't he? He's what, shy. I'd call him shy, wouldn't you, Marge?

MARGE: Well, sometimes – yes. I suppose he has been.

COLIN: Big men are like that. They're always shy.

PAUL: I'm not shy.

DIANA: You're not very big.

PAUL: I'm fairly big.

MARGE: You're not as big as Gordon.

PAUL: Nobody's as big as Gordon.

[*Pause.*]

MARGE: That's because I feed him. When his stomach's not playing him up.

COLIN: Gordon was famous for his appetite.

MARGE: He still is. I like a man with an appetite.

COLIN: There you are, you see. Two more satisfied customers.

[*Pause.* COLIN *laughs.*]

DIANA: What?

COLIN: Sorry. No, I was just remembering something.

DIANA: What?

COLIN: It was just something me and Carol – it wouldn't interest you.

DIANA: Go on.

COLIN: No, no . . .

MARGE: Go on. We want to hear about her.

COLIN: Well, it was just one of those fantastic moments, you know.

MARGE [*romantic*]: Ah . . .

COLIN: It was – well – when we first knew each other and – I forgot where it was now – I think we were walking across the common – there was nobody about – and she suddenly turned to me and she said 'Colin, I think I'm ready to let you kiss me now. I'd like that very much. Would you, please?'

MARGE: Ah . . .

COLIN: And after I'd kissed her, I remember I was over the moon, literally. You should have seen me, I was singing and dancing and leaping about all over that common . . .

MARGE: Ah . . .

DIANA: Ah . . .

EVELYN: Huh.

[*Slight pause.*]

PAUL: Have you given any thought as to who's going to win the League this year, Colin?

COLIN: No, not really, no.

PAUL: I rather fancy our lot this year. They're going rather well ...

JOHN: They are.

COLIN: Well, I still follow them. What was it? Four nil last Saturday. Did you go?

PAUL: No. Yes.

COLIN: Sounded a cracker.

PAUL: It was.

DIANA: There's nothing much can come between Paul and a football game, is there, Paul? Now come on, I want all these eaten up or I won't cut the cake.

MARGE: Well, if you've got any left I'll take it home to Gordon in a bag.

PAUL: Oh my God.

COLIN: It's a wonderful spread, Di. Really wonderful. Right up to standard.

DIANA: Thank you.

COLIN: Di's teas. Famous. I remember having a few of those over the years. Don't you, Paul?

PAUL: Eh?

COLIN: Remember when we used to go round to tea? To Di and her sister Barbara's?

PAUL: Oh yes.

COLIN: Every weekend. Mind you, Paul was in such a state, he could never eat it though. He'd say to me, how the hell am I supposed to sit down opposite a fantastic looking girl like that and be expected to eat anything. That's the last thing on my mind. He really had it bad.

DIANA: For Barbara?

COLIN: Barbara? Come off it. For you.

DIANA: Oh.

PAUL: No, I didn't.

COLIN: Look, he's shy. He's gone shy. Big men, I told you. Tell her about the table napkin.

PAUL: Shut up.

COLIN: All right. I'll tell them. We used to go round to tea, you see, to their house – did I ever tell you this, John?

JOHN: Don't think so.

PAUL: Look, Colin –

DIANA: Shut up, Paul, I want to hear.

MARGE: We want to hear.

COLIN: I think it was, well, practically the first time we went round to Barbara, Di and her mother's for tea and Paul was – well, he was sweating – literally sweating and all the way there he kept saying – what am I going to say to her – this was to Di. And when he got there, the girls and their mother had laid out this tea, all properly, you know. Table napkins, everything correct . . .

PAUL: Look, this was a long time ago.

COLIN: That's why I'm telling them.

DIANA: Shut up.

COLIN: Anyway, the first thing that happens, Paul and I are in the front room there, waiting – they're all out in the kitchen, giggling away, getting the tea ready – and Paul, well you know what he can be like, he gets so nervous, he's pacing up and down, sits down, gets up, sits down and then finally he leans against the wall with one hand – like this, you see – [*he demonstrates.*] and he puts his hand right on one of those ducks. China ducks, you know, the sort people have flying up their wall. A row of them, you know. Anyway, he puts his hand on one of them and crack – bang goes one duck. So there he is, he's standing there with half a duck in each hand and we hear them coming back. No time to do anything. So he sits down to tea with his pockets full of duck.

[*They laugh.*]

There we are, sitting all through this tea waiting for someone

to look up and say – hallo – one, two – what's happened to
him. He must have migrated.

[*They all laugh again.*]

DIANA: We never missed it.

COLIN: No, well. He took it home, glued it together and hung it
up again when we came next week.

DIANA: Typical.

COLIN: He was so worried, he could hardly keep his eyes on Di.
Anyway, at the end of the meal, do you know what he did –
and this shows how romantic he is underneath all that lot – he
picked up that napkin that you'd been using, Di, and he put it
in his pocket. Took it home to remind him of you.

MARGE: Ah.

DIANA: Is that where it went?

PAUL: I don't remember doing that.

MARGE: I think that's a lovely story. Just shows. All men are
romantics at heart.

[*Pause.*]

JOHN: I never did that sort of thing.

EVELYN: You nicked my Uncle's screwdriver.

JOHN: I did not.

EVELYN: He saw you taking it. He said if he comes round here
again, I'll break his neck.

JOHN: You never invited me for tea.

EVELYN: You never sat down for long enough.

DIANA: Now then. More tea?

COLIN: Please.

PAUL [*laughing suddenly*]: You know something, Col?

COLIN: What?

PAUL: I've just remembered. I've still got that table napkin of
hers, you know.

COLIN: Have you really?

PAUL: Yes. I use it to clean the car with.

[DIANA *picks up the cream jug and pours it slowly over*
PAUL's *head.* PAUL *sits for a moment, stunned.*]

[*Leaping up*] Hey! What are you doing, woman?

MARGE: Di –!

COLIN: Hey, hey!

JOHN: Oy!

DIANA: Oh, I'm so sorry.

PAUL [*outraged*]: What are you doing?

DIANA: I am so sorry.

PAUL: You poured that all over me. She poured that over me.

MARGE: I'll get a cloth.

PAUL: No, I can't use a cloth. I'll have to wash it out.

MARGE: Not for you. For the chair.

[MARGE *goes out to the kitchen.*]

PAUL: Bloody woman's off her head. She poured it all over me.

[PAUL *stamps off upstairs.*]

DIANA: Accidents will happen.

COLIN: Well . . . [*He laughs awkwardly.*]

DIANA: I'm sorry, Colin. You were saying?

COLIN: Was I?

DIANA: You'll have to excuse my husband, Colin, he's changed
over the years . . . Now then, tea for you, John?

JOHN: Er – thank you.

DIANA: Pass your cup. Evelyn?

EVELYN: No.

DIANA: Thank you.

EVELYN: Thank you.

COLIN: Well, I daresay we've all changed in some ways.

DIANA: Possibly. Some more than most.

[MARGE *returns with a cloth, bowl of water and paper towels.*]

MARGE: Would it be all right to use this for it, Di?

[*Indicates cloth.*]

DIANA: Just as you like.

MARGE: Look, paper towels. Very useful. [*Examining the
damage.*] Oh, it's not too bad.

[MARGE *sets to work.* DIANA *hands* COLIN *his tea. Then*
JOHN.]

DIANA: Is that strong enough for you, Colin?

COLIN: Oh, that's lovely, Di. That's perfect. Perfect. [*Laughing.*] Just the way Carol used to make it.

DIANA: You can't say fairer than that, can you.

COLIN: Listen Di. . .

DIANA: John . . . .

[*Slight pause.*]

COLIN: Listen, Di . . . Just now, I think what Paul said just now – it may have sounded to you a bit – er – well – I think, actually, I understand what he was feeling. I know what was going through his mind. I embarrassed him with that story – I shouldn't have told it and – er – well, Paul, basically – here I go again. I told you I'm a Paul expert . . .

DIANA: So am I, Colin. So am I.

COLIN: Yes, right, point taken, surely. But . . . you see, Paul is really a very romantic man. He's soft. I've known him a long time – oh, he'll give you that old gruff bit – and the 'I don't care what anyone thinks' bit – but honestly, Di, you know yourself, he's ashamed of his own nature, you see. Somewhere, he's got this idea that if he shows any sort of gentleness to people they'll think he's soft. And of course, that's what's made him the success he is today. Let's face it. Because he's managed to cover it up. And I think that in some ways you'd be the first to say thank heavens he has. I mean. You've got this marvellous house, full of lovely things, you've got two fine children and – well, let's be fair, you've got just about everything a human being could ask for. And it's a very very sad fact of life that you don't get any of that through being soft. That's why people like me, John, Gordon, we're never going to get in the same bracket as Paul. Never. No, Di, I'm afraid the only thing left for you is to love him for what he is. Right, John?

JOHN: Right. Right.

COLIN: Marge?

MARGE [*not quite convinced*]: Yes . . .

[*Pause.*]

EVELYN: Do you happen to write for these magazines by any chance?

COLIN: Eh?

[*Pause.* MARGE *finishes her task.*]

MARGE: I think that's done it. Shall I do over the rest while I'm here, Di? [*She laughs.*]

[MARGE *goes out.*]

JOHN: You pleased with that car of yours?

COLIN: Yes. Yes, it gets me about.

JOHN: I've always fancied the look of those. The only thing that worries me about it is, is it slightly under-powered?

EVELYN: I bet it's got a carpet that fits.

COLIN: No, it seems to be okay. It's not a racer – but –

JOHN: No, no, quite. I think I'll consider getting one sometime.

EVELYN: A cheap one with no wheels.

JOHN: Oh, lay off, Evelyn. There's a good girl. I spend my days slaving for her – slaving . . .

[MARGE *returns.*]

MARGE: There we are. All done. I think I've earned a spot more tea, haven't I, Di?

[DIANA *is in a trance of her own.*]

Di?

DIANA: It's all yours.

MARGE: Oh, righto.

[MARGE *pours herself a cup of tea and sits in silence.*]

DIANA [*quietly at first*]: When I was a little girl, you know, my sister Barbara was very jealous of me because Mother bought me this coat for my birthday . . .

MARGE: Oh, really?

DIANA: I'd seen it in the window of this shop when I walked to school. It was red with one of those little collars and then trimmed round the neck and the sleeves. I used to pass it every day. They'd put it on this window dummy. A little child dummy. It was a really pretty dummy. Not like some of them.

A proper face. It had very very blue eyes and sort of ash coloured hair, quite short and it was standing in the middle of this sort of false grass. I wanted that coat so much. And Barbara used to say, you'll never get Mother to buy you that. But I did. And on my birthday, I put it on and I felt, oh, so happy you can't imagine. And then we were all going for a walk and we were just going out and I happened to catch sight of myself full length in the mirror in the hall. And I looked like nothing on earth in it. I looked terrible.

MARGE: Oh dear.

COLIN: What a shame.

DIANA: Yes, it was. I wanted a red one especially. Because I had this burning ambition, you see, to join the Canadian Royal Mounted Police.

MARGE: Good gracious ...

DIANA: People used to say 'You can't join the Mounted Police. You're a little girl. Little girls don't join the Mounted Police. Little girls do nice things like typing and knitting and nursing and having babies.' So I married Paul instead. Because they refused to let me join the Mounted Police. I married him because he kept asking me. And because people kept saying that it would be a much nicer thing to do than ... and so I did. And I learnt my typing and I had my babies and I looked after them for as long as they'd let me and then suddenly I realized I'd been doing all the wrong things. They'd been wrong telling me to marry Paul and have babies, if they're not even going to let you keep them, and I should have joined the Mounted Police, that's what I should have done. I know I should have joined the Mounted Police. [*Starting to sob.*] I want to join the Mounted Police. Please ... [*She starts to sob louder and louder till they become a series of short staccato screams.*]

MARGE: John, for heaven's sake. Get Paul down here.

JOHN: Paul. Yes, I'll get Paul ...

[JOHN *goes to the stairs and out.* EVELYN *has risen and is studying* DIANA *with curiosity.*]

EVELYN: What's the matter with her?

MARGE: Get out of my way. [*Shaking* DIANA.] Di – Di – Di . . .

   [PAUL *comes back with* JOHN *behind him.* PAUL's *hair is still wet from washing it.*]

PAUL: What's wrong? What's the matter with her?

MARGE: She's not well, Paul. You'll have to get a doctor.

PAUL: Di – Di, come on now . . .

JOHN: Shall I get her some water?

PAUL: No, we'll get her up to bed. We'll get a doctor. Give me a hand, John.

JOHN: Right.

MARGE: I'll get a cold cloth. That'll help.

   [MARGE *runs out to kitchen.*]

   [JOHN *and* PAUL *try to lift* DIANA *by each arm.*]

DIANA [*fighting* PAUL *away*]: Get away from me . . .

PAUL: Now, Di . . .

DIANA: Get away!

COLIN [*who has retreated in horror to the far corner of the room, ineffectually*]: Can I . . .?

EVELYN: I'll do it. Here.

   [*She takes hold of* DIANA's *arm, the one that* PAUL *has relinquished.* JOHN *still has hold of the other arm.*]

DIANA [*thrusting* EVELYN *away with some violence*]: Get away from me, you bitch . . .

   [MARGE *returns with a flannel.*]

JOHN: It's no good. She won't let anybody – [*struggling with her.*] – help her.

MARGE: Here, hold this. [*She thrusts the flannel into* COLIN's *hand.*]

COLIN: Wah!

MARGE: Come along, out of the way.

JOHN: We could try slapping her face.

57

MARGE: No, we couldn't. How would you like your face slapped? Don't be silly. Come along, Di, that's it . . .

[MARGE *and* JOHN *between them start to steer* DIANA *to the door.*]

COLIN: Can I be of any . . .?

MARGE: It's all right, Colin, sit down. Easy with her, John, that's it . . . I'll phone the doctor from upstairs, Paul.

PAUL: Right.

MARGE: You're still with Harris, aren't you?

PAUL: Yes.

MARGE: Come along, John. She needs support. Support her.

JOHN: I'm trying to support her. She's bloody heavy.

[JOHN, DIANA *and* MARGE *go out. A silence. The men stand awkwardly.* EVELYN *sits and picks her nails.*]

PAUL: What started that?

COLIN: I don't really know. She just started talking about the Mounted Police.

PAUL: The what?

COLIN: The Royal Canadian Mounted Police. She seemed to want to join them.

PAUL [*shaking his head*]: Well . . . [*He sits.*]

COLIN: There's something very wrong there, Paul. Very wrong indeed.

[MARGE *returns busily.*]

PAUL: Can you manage?

MARGE: It's all right. She's just been a little bit ill on the stairs. Nothing serious. Evelyn.

EVELYN: What?

MARGE: Paper towels. In the kitchen. Come on, this is partly your fault. You get them and clean it up.

[MARGE *goes out.*]

[EVELYN *clicks her tongue and goes off into the kitchen.*]

COLIN: Have you had this trouble before, Paul?

PAUL: Not quite like this.

COLIN: Worrying.

PAUL: Right.

COLIN: I think you should go up with her, you know. She probably needs you.

PAUL: Oh come on, Colin ...

COLIN: What?

PAUL: You heard her. She doesn't want me within twenty yards of her.

COLIN: Oh yes, but that was ... she was hysterical. I mean –

PAUL: I'm the last person.

[EVELYN *enters from the kitchen clutching a handful of paper towels.*]

EVELYN: This is a right cheery afternoon this is. His lordship's bawling his head off out there as well ...

[*She goes off to the hall.*]

COLIN: I remember when Carol had flu. She wouldn't let go of my hand. Except to turn over. I sat with her for two nights in a row. But then I think the thing with Carol and me was –

PAUL: Col.

COLIN: Yes?

PAUL: Do me a favour. Just shut up for one minute about Carol, would you. I don't want to hurt your feelings but – not just at the moment ...

COLIN: Oh, I'm sorry. I was – just thinking it – might help, you know.

PAUL: No, Colin. Really and truly, I don't honestly think it does. I mean, you and Carol were – something quite different, weren't you?

COLIN: Yes, I realize that, yes. [*He thinks for a moment.*] All the same, you're wrong, you know.

PAUL: How come?

COLIN: Di didn't mean that. That she didn't want you near her.

PAUL: She convinced me.

COLIN [*laughing*]: No, no I'm sorry, Paul, you're not fooling anyone, you know. Neither's Di. Remember me? I'm the one that used to sit and talk to her for days and nights on end in the old days. Do you know what we talked about, constantly and incessantly?

PAUL [*wearily*]: Go on, amaze me . . .

COLIN: You. All you. I mean, at one time, when she used to ask me round a lot, I used to think, Hallo, I'm on to a good thing here. Can't be bad. Must mean something. And we'd sit down all evening, in her front room, drink coffee and talk about you all the time. Well, after a bit, I began to get the message. It wasn't me she was after at all. You . . . Only you were out with her sister Barbara. No, you're number one in Di's book, Paul. Always have been. I don't think you realize quite what a pedestal that woman has set you upon. She'd follow you to the ends of the earth, you know.

PAUL: She probably would at that.

COLIN: I hope you realize what you've got there?

PAUL: I do, I do.

COLIN: Stick with it, Paul, old mate.

PAUL: Thank you, Colin. Thank you very much.

COLIN: I know you will. I know you. [*Pause.*] You know something? The one regret I'll always have? That Carol and I – our relationship – can never develop now into the sort of relationship you and Di must have . . .

PAUL: Oh, Colin . . .

COLIN: Never mind. Too late now. You feeling a bit brighter?

PAUL: Oh Colin, what are we going to do with you?

COLIN: Me? [*He laughs.*] That's the last thing to worry about. Mind you, I'm glad I came round this afternoon. I don't know how you lot ever managed without me, eh?

[COLIN *laughs.* PAUL *laughs.* COLIN *stops laughing.* PAUL *continues. It's hysterical, almost manic, uncontrollable laughter.* COLIN *becomes concerned.* EVELYN *enters. She stares at* PAUL.]

EVELYN: Oh. I'm going to fetch Wayne in. It's raining . . .

[EVELYN *goes out through the kitchen.*]

[PAUL *finally stops laughing.*]

PAUL: I'm sorry, Col ... sorry ...

COLIN: All right?

PAUL: Yes, yes ...

[*JOHN enters.*]

JOHN: Right. Marge gave her one of her sleeping pills. If that doesn't get her to sleep, she says she'll phone the doctor.

PAUL: Thanks.

JOHN: Not at all, not at all. [*Looking around.*] Has she gone home?

PAUL: No, she's with the baby.

JOHN: Ah. Sorry about that, Col old mate.

COLIN: Oh –

JOHN: Doesn't happen every day.

COLIN: I hope not.

JOHN: You must come to our house next time. Absolute peace. Neither of us ever says a word to each other. That's the secret of a successful union. Marry a strong silent woman like Evelyn ... [*He shadow-boxes.*] Bam – bam ... [*At the table.*] Isn't anyone going to finish these?

PAUL: Help yourself.

[*JOHN munches a sandwich.*]

COLIN: I must be off soon, Paul. Don't want to be in the way, you know.

[*PAUL, brooding, makes no reply.*]

JOHN [*munching*]: The good thing about Evelyn – and she has her good side, although she is most careful to hide it from strangers – is that she has absolutely no sense of humour. Which is very useful since it means you never have to waste your time trying to cheer her up. Because she's permanently unhappy. Misery is her natural state. We are also fortunate in being blessed with a very miserable boy. In fact, apart from me, we are the most miserable family you are ever likely to meet and I'm working on me. Am I keeping you awake?

PAUL: Sit down.

JOHN [*sitting*]: What do you think about that deal? Worth a try.

PAUL: I don't know.

JOHN: A hundred and twenty-five per cent. Worth a try.

PAUL: I'll think about it.

[*The phone rings.*]

Answer that, will you, John.

JOHN [*doing so*]: Hallo ... could you speak up? Gordon? ... hallo, Gordon, matey ... it's John, yes ... yes, she's here ... wait a minute ... I'll give her a yell.

COLIN [*moving to the door*]: I'll call her.

PAUL: Tell her she can take it upstairs.

JOHN [*still listening at phone*]: Hang on, Col, she's here ... you got it then, Marge ... okay ... she's got it ... [*He goes to place the receiver and then, covering the mouthpiece, listens in. He laughs.*]

PAUL: Put it down.

JOHN [*enjoying himself*]: Hang on, hang on.

COLIN: Tell her I'd like a word with him when she's –

JOHN [*laughing*]: He's burst his hot water bottle. [*Listens.*] He's in a shocking state.

PAUL: Put it down.

JOHN: You should hear –

PAUL: It's private, put it down.

[JOHN *does so, reluctantly.*]

COLIN: I wanted a word with him.

JOHN: I don't think you would at the moment. He's a moaner, isn't he? A real moaner. Big fat moaner. Old gloom Gordon.

COLIN: He was a great left-arm bowler.

JOHN: Oh, yes. Could have played for the County.

COLIN: Easily.

JOHN: Till he wrecked his shoulder.

COLIN: Tragic, that.

JOHN: Yes. We could do with a good left-arm bowler in this County.

COLIN: He had his heart set on that as a career, didn't he?

JOHN: Yes. What is he now? Fire prevention officer, married to Marge and fat.

COLIN: I think she's very good for him, don't you?

JOHN: Yes, she's all right. I don't know how good he is for her, though. [*He lifts the phone off the hook to listen for a second.*]

PAUL [*wearily*]: What are you doing?

JOHN [*laughing*]: He's shouting his head off at her still . . . [*He stays listening and pulls a face at what he hears.*]

COLIN [*moving to him*]: John . . . excuse me . . . do you mind? . . . Thank you . . . [*He takes the phone from* JOHN.]

JOHN [*startled*]: What are you doing?

COLIN [*into phone*]: Hallo . . . hallo . . . Marge . . . Gordon . . . Sorry if this is a private conversation . . . pardon me for butting in . . . Colin here . . . Hallo, Jumbo . . . Excuse me, Marge . . . Just wanted to say, get well soon . . . pecker up . . . I expect Marge'll be home to look after you shortly, won't you, Marge? You've got a real treasure there, Gordon, a real treasure . . . God bless . . . won't talk any longer . . . Back to nurse Marge . . . Bye-bye . . . bye-bye, Gordon . . . [*He replaces the receiver.*] That's nice. Managed a quick word, anyway . . . [*He smiles.*]

PAUL: Oh, my God . . .

JOHN: How was he?

COLIN: Between you and me, I don't think he's too good. Marge sounded very cut up. Very cut up indeed.

[EVELYN *pushes the baby in.*]

JOHN: You bringing him in?

EVELYN: It's raining out there.

JOHN: Rain won't hurt him. Good for him. Make him grow.

EVELYN: He's nearly off again, anyway.

COLIN: May I have a look?

EVELYN: Yes. Just don't make daft noises at him. He doesn't like it.

COLIN [*looking into pram*]: Oh, great. He's so – small, isn't he?

EVELYN: Yes. Look at him, little devil, he's really fighting to stay awake.

COLIN: He's just great. The feeling you both must have, looking at him . . . must make you so . . .

EVELYN [*cutting him short*]: He's not bad. [*She rocks the pram. To* JOHN.] We're going in a minute.

JOHN: Right.

COLIN: Yes, as soon as Marge comes down, I think I must . . .

JOHN: You all right, Paul?

PAUL: Fine. I must go up in a minute. I've got a lot of work to do upstairs.

[MARGE *comes in, blowing her nose.*]

MARGE: She's nearly off to sleep. I think she'll be all right when she's rested.

COLIN: Ah, yes. Sleep. A great healer. [*Confidentially.*] Hope you didn't mind me butting in on the phone call just now, Marge?

MARGE: That's all right, Colin.

COLIN: Thought as he was on, I'd have a quick word with him.

MARGE: Lovely.

COLIN: He sounded a bit . . . er . . . under the weather . . .

MARGE: He's all right.

COLIN: Not his usual cheery old self.

MARGE: He's all right.

COLIN: Sounded as if he could do with a bit of jollying up . . .

MARGE [*more sharply*]: He'll be perfectly all right the minute I get back to him, don't worry, Colin.

COLIN: Ah, well. That's good.

[PAUL *sits with his eyes closed.*]

[EVELYN *rocks the pram.*]

[JOHN *gazes out of the window.*]

[MARGE *stands wrapped in thought.*]

Well. [*Pause.*] I suppose I ought to be . . . Much as I'd like to . . . Making tracks and all that.

[*Pause.*]

COLIN: Yes.

[*Pause.*]

[*Looking at his watch.*] Good heavens, yes. Look at the . . . It's a long drive. I'd better make a start. [*Pause.*] Good-bye, all . . .

MARGE [*coming out of her reverie*]: Oh, Colin, are you off?

COLIN: Yes, I think I'd . . .

MARGE: Yes. Don't forget your photographs . . .

COLIN: Oh, no. I wouldn't do that. Not likely to do that.

MARGE: I hope you – manage all right, Colin.

COLIN: Me? Oh, I'm fine. I've always fallen on my feet, you know . . . I've still got a good job – health and strength – and lately, I think I've found a few good friends over there as well. Carol's parents, to name but two. I'm always round with them these days. You know, talking over old times and things. And if I really get a bit depressed, out come the old albums. It's a pity you didn't meet her, Marge. You'd have got on like a house on fire.

MARGE: Yes, I'm sure.

COLIN: Well. Good-bye, Evelyn. Been a great pleasure meeting you.

EVELYN: Bye.

JOHN: Cheerio, old Col. See you.

COLIN: You bet. Come over and see me.

JOHN: Might just do that. When I get the new car. Have a few – [*drinking gesture.*] . . . together.

COLIN: Any time, Paul.

PAUL: Bye, Colin. Take care.

COLIN: And you. Say good-bye to Di, will you?

PAUL: Oh, sure. She'll be sorry she missed you.

COLIN: Bye-bye, Marge. No, it's all right, I'll see myself out. [*Hesitating.*] Er – I really appreciated you all inviting me over here this afternoon, you know and, well . . . thanks a lot. You've really been great. All of you.

MARGE: Good-bye, Colin. And I hope perhaps, you know –

later on – you'll . . . once you've got over . . . I mean, I know it will be difficult for a time for you to forget about Carol . . .

COLIN: Forget her? Oh come on, Marge. You know me better than that, don't you? [*Smiling round.*] Bye-bye, all.

[COLIN *goes out. A pause.*]

MARGE: He's a nice boy, isn't he?

JOHN: Good old Col. Just the same.

MARGE: Paul, I'll have to go home to Gordon in a minute.

PAUL: Yes. Fine, Marge. Fine. You do that . . .

MARGE: But if by any chance you need help – with her – you know my number. As soon as I've cleaned Gordon up, I can easily look back.

PAUL: No, we'll manage, Marge, honestly.

MARGE: She should sleep now.

[EVELYN *starts singing, still rocking the pram.*]

[PAUL *sits and starts to doze.*]

JOHN [*who has sat down for once*]: I'll cut that carpet up for the car tomorrow.

MARGE [*sitting down herself for a moment*]: I don't think I'd better leave Gordon on his own again when he's ill, you know. He doesn't like it. He prefers it if I'm there. [*Slight pause.*] Oh, it's terrible. I haven't got the energy to move now. Once I've sat down . . . I think those shoes will go with that coat. I hope so . . . oh, look at us. Honestly. All drooping about like wet weekends . . . still, why shouldn't we, I say. There are worse ways of spending the time. Than sitting peacefully with your friends. Nice to sit with your friends now and again. Nice . . .

[EVELYN *continues her singing.*]

[MARGE *daydreams.*]

[PAUL *starts to snore loudly.*]

[JOHN *jiggles.*]

CURTAIN

Glossary: reading the text

Act I

1 **open plan**   large and spacious with no artificial dividers.

   executive-style   suggesting the house is modern and expensive, such as a well-to-do business-person's family might live in.

   wrought iron   fancy iron work used to make various household items.

   in lieu   instead of.

   frosted glass   a patterned glass, difficult to see through, specially manufactured to obscure objects.

   Parquet   wooden strips arranged in patterns as a floor covering.

   fraught   anxious, distressed.

   cherubims   heavenly angels with chubby human faces.

2 **squash**   indoor ball game played with rackets and a small rubber ball.

9 **Jumjums**   a babyish term of affection.

17 **tart**   (slang) abusive term for a woman who 'sleeps around'.

18 **Yellow Pages**   a telephone directory listing in alphabetical order all types of domestic and commercial services and businesses; here used sarcastically as a long list.

24 **the flower pot men**   a reference to the children's television programme which ran from 1952–71 called **The Flower Pot Men** about two string puppet men, Bill and Ben, who lived in flower pots in a garden, looked identical and spoke in very silly voices.

   patently   obviously, clearly.

34 *disinterested*   not really interested in, not listening.

41 *bemused*   puzzled.

---

1   What is revealed about Diana and her relationship with Paul from the stage directions and her opening conversations with Evelyn and Marge?

2   How does Marge try to keep the peace in this act and how would you describe her character?

3   What comic devices does Ayckbourn use to depict the marriages of Diana/Paul and Evelyn/John?

4   What are the various stages of the tensions between all the characters by the time Colin arrives?

5   Explain the connections between all the characters and Colin.

6   How do the different characters react to Colin when he arrives? Have they changed from the way they were when they were talking about him *before* he made an appearance?

Act 2

46 *The bees knees*   expression meaning someone who is particularly admirable or good at something.

per se   (Latin) in itself.

56 *Canadian Royal Mounted Police*   Canadian horse-back police, with a very distinctive uniform.

62 *left-arm bowler*   referring to Gordon as a cricketer.

1 What have you learned about Gordon?

2 What do you think causes Diana's long outbursts about her childhood memories and dreams?

3 How do Colin's comments about Paul, Diana, John, Marge and Gordon emphasise both the sad and funny sides of their relationships?

4 What is revealed about the past of Paul and Diana?

5 What is important about the characters not seen (Carol and Gordon)?

6 How far do you think Colin is a sympathetic character? Describe his relationship with Carol.

7 Which characters are most affected by the afternoon tea party? Explain the reasons for your choice.

Study programme

Characters

As you read the play remember, when you shape your views about each character, to consider:

- what the character does, and how he or she behaves towards others in different situations;
- what the character says, when and to whom;
- what others say about the character;
- what stage directions are given about the character.

Diana

1 Look at this list of adjectives to describe Diana:

kind   concerned   nervous   anxious   angry
shy   deceived   paranoid   generous   friendly
sincere

Find examples from the play for each of these. Add more if you think there are some other aspects to her character not already listed.

2 Alan Ayckbourn was once asked about the effect on the audience of Diana's hysterical outburst in Act Two (pages 55–6), about always wanting to have been a member of the Canadian Mounted Police and whether this moment upset anyone. He replied:

> *It never came as a horrid shock because something had been bubbling towards that all evening. The tensions had been there and, in a sense, one is prepared for such events by the presence, in the middle, of the*

awful Colin slowly accelerating any imminent crisis with his platitudes and words of goodwill.

Plays and Players, September 1975

Choose four other points in the play where the audience becomes aware of the stresses and strains in Diana's life.

- Think about her words and the way she reacts with each of the other characters.

- Explain how they reveal something more about Diana's character.

- Look at the way Diana deals with these situations and awkward moments.

3 Re-read Diana's long speech (pages 2–3) from 'No, there are times when I think that's the principal trouble between Paul and me ...' to '... I expect them, both of them, at least to have some feeling for me.'

In pairs, summarise all her *main points*. Then, based on what you find, one of you present the positive side of Diana's marriage to Paul and the other present the negative aspects.

4 Using the notes you have made, write a character study of Diana of about 500 words or more. Check your work and redraft it, using some quotations from the play to help your main points.

Colin

5 This is what Diana says to Marge about Colin:

> *I mean, we're still his friends. I doubt if he's got any where he is now because it takes him ages to get to know people ... He'll need his friends.*

page 11

Later in the play Colin says:

> ... I'm glad I came round this afternoon. I don't know how you lot ever managed without me, eh?
>
> page 60

and

> I really appreciated you all inviting me over here, this afternoon, you know and, well ... thanks a lot. You've really been great. All of you.
>
> page 65

Think about the effects Colin has on the other characters.

- What are these effects?
- How are the lives of the other characters changed by his visit?
- The term 'catalyst' is used in science to describe a chemical which changes other chemicals but which remains the same itself. What examples can you find which show Colin to be a catalyst?

6
> Colin has gained this immunity [of being affected by a crisis] through having been touched by tragedy. He's like a man you've always detested being suddenly struck with an incurable disease; as everyone knows he only has six months to live, gestures of courtesy and tolerance are offered when, in normal circumstances, a fourpenny one would have been forthcoming. Colin's immunity is something he doesn't really deserve.
>
> **Plays and Players**, September 1995

What Ayckbourn had to say about Colin in this interview may seem very harsh. After all he is not a 'bad' man. He means well throughout. The drama critic Michael Billington, in his discussion of the irony of the play, refers to Colin as a great theatrical device – 'the sentimental man':

> Ayckbourn triggers off disaster through a well-meaning, bereaved friend who assiduously rakes over everyone's past. Colin's motives are the kindest possible. The effects are calamitous ... It is part of Ayckbourn's

craft that Colin not only gets everyone wrong: he also precipitates dramatic crisis with ... bonhomie ... The audience rejoices ... Colin ... is myopically unaware of the havoc he is creating.

Macmillan Modern Dramatists: Alan Ayckbourn

In pairs, prepare speeches arguing *for* and *against* the statement 'Colin is a man to detest'. Look carefully at Colin's long speeches in Act Two.

The other characters

7 A lot is said about Paul by Diana and Evelyn when he is not on stage. Colin talks about Paul and past events in his presence. The audience hears about the good and bad sides to his character. Prepare a two-minute talk, in rôle, as Paul defending your actions in the play and in the past.

8 Why do you think the character of Marge is important? How does she help the other characters during the afternoon?

9 Gordon is never seen or heard in the play but he is often described and has telephone conversations in which the audience hears the responses from Marge, Colin and John (pages 9–10, 26–7, 62–3).

Choose two of these telephone conversations and write Gordon's part in it. Now write out the whole transcript of the conversation as a play between Gordon and the people with whom he is speaking.

Look carefully at all the descriptions and comments about Gordon (his various ailments, his size, his attitude towards children and so on) throughout the play to help make your work faithful to the character.

Then act out the telephone conversations.

10 Imagine John or Evelyn write a detailed letter about their marriage difficulties and complain about their spouse to a problem page in one of the magazines Evelyn reads.

Write the letter and the magazine's reply.

II Letters between Colin and Carol are found with Carol's diary. Write some of those letters and a few diary extracts from the fourteen months Carol and Colin knew each other.

Themes

1 *So much can go wrong in a marriage. The worst kind of marriage is the one where second-best has been settled for, where no attempt is made to even <u>approach</u> the problems. That's awful ... I have great sympathy for people like Diana in* **Absent Friends**, *desperately trying to make marriage work. The women in this ... play, in fact are probably drawn more sympathetically than are the men. And that puts the record straight, because most plays about marriage tend to get written from the man's point of view.*

Alan Ayckbourn, **Plays and Players**, September 1975

In a group of four, examine the marriages of Diana and Paul, John and Evelyn, Marge and Gordon, and the engagement of Colin and Carol.

Look carefully, not just at how the couples appear to get on but also at what is said about their relationships by themselves and by other people.

2 In Willy Russell's **Shirley Valentine**, like Ayckbourn, the playwright is sympathetic towards the women in the play. The main character talks about her marriage (often with her kitchen wall as her only audience!). These two short speeches are said alone and directly into the camera:

He says he still loves me. You know. He doesn't. It's just somethin' he says. It's funny isn't it, 'I love you'. Like it makes everythin' all right. Like

74

you can be beaten and battered and half insane – and if you complain he'll say, 'What's wrong? You know I love you.'

And I know what you're thinkin'. Why don't I leave him? Well, I'm terrified if you want to know. I'm terrified that if I left him there would be nowhere for me to go. No place for me in the life beyond the wall.
Shirley Valentine, Longman Literature, pages 35–36

Use these comments from **Shirley Valentine** to brainstorm and compare the way marriage is presented in **Absent Friends**. You need to think about the difficulties and joys for both men and women in the marriages portrayed.

Share your ideas, think about references and quotations which would be helpful and then use your ideas to plan an essay entitled 'The way marriage is presented in **Absent Friends**'.

3 In **Absent Friends** there are contrasting views about death:

- MARGE I don't think he'll want to talk about Carol.
  JOHN No?
  MARGE I shouldn't think so. He'll want to forget.
  JOHN I hope so. I hate death. Gives me the creeps.
  EVELYN Get on.
  JOHN It does.
  EVELYN You?
  JOHN I get all ... uggghhh. (*He shudders*) Don't talk about it.
  EVELYN (*laughs*) Death, death, death.
  JOHN Shut up.

  pages 19–20

- COLIN ... I don't know if you've ever met a perfect person. But that's what she was ... And I, me, I'd had the love of a perfect person. And that's something I can always be grateful for ... Because I've been denied my own happiness, I don't envy or begrudge you yours. I just want you to know that, despite everything that happened, in a funny sort of way, I too am very happy.

  page 40

How do the various different characters respond to death throughout the play?

4 What points do you think Alan Ayckbourn is making by choosing the serious, sometimes taboo, subject of death for a comedy? How do you think he manages to write a comedy about such a serious subject?

5 The play looks at different types of friendship:

> PAUL Fat lot of comfort he'll get here.
>
> MARGE We can try. It'll only be for an hour.
>
> JOHN As long as he doesn't start talking about death, I don't mind. If he starts on about death or dying, I'm off.
>
> EVELYN I don't know why you came.
>
> JOHN Well – like Di says, it's – friendly.
>
> EVELYN You don't like him.
>
> JOHN Colin? I don't mind him.
>
> EVELYN You said you didn't like him.
>
> JOHN I didn't mind him.
>
> PAUL I didn't like him.
>
> DIANA You went round with him enough.
>
> PAUL I did not.

pages 23–4

This extract seems to justify the old statement – with friends like these, who needs enemies?! The irony is reinforced when Colin says later on in the play:

> ... I've had what a lot of people would probably give their right arm for – friends. Real friends, like John and Paul and Gordon and Di.

page 40

Which examples of the good and bad aspects of friendship can you find in the play? What do you think Ayckbourn is showing his audience about friendship?

6 The phrase 'absent friends' is usually associated with a gathering of people raising a glass and remembering those who are not present, either because they could not attend or because they are not alive. Why do you think Alan Ayckbourn chose to call his play *Absent Friends*?

7 The English tea party is an old custom and ritual. Think of as many reasons as possible as to why this setting works so well in this play.

Style and language

1 In pairs, devise two separate charts – one highlighting some of the comic moments in the play, the other showing the serious ones. Use references from the text where possible. Then compare your notes. You may find that the same incidents or lines are in both charts. Discuss what this reveals about Ayckbourn's craft as a writer.

2 What kinds of comedy can be found in *Absent Friends*? The following list will help you identify the techniques used by Alan Ayckbourn:

- **Situation comedy**: a term used to describe a light-hearted look at everyday life and the humorous effects of people's actions.
  For example, Marge's telephone conversation with Gordon about his problem of having spilt cough mixture in bed (pages 9–10).

- **Deflation**: when something dramatic is expected but expectations are reversed (a bit like pumping up a balloon and then letting the air out).
  For example, when Diana talks about the red coat she craved as a child and then, at the end of her long speech, reveals how terrible she looked in it (pages 55–6).

- **Sarcasm**: saying something when really the opposite is meant. For example, when John says:

   You must come to our house next time. Absolute peace. Neither of us ever says a word to each other.

   page 61

   This can also have the effect of deflation and irony.

- **Character**: using what an audience knows about a character or description of a character for humorous effect. For example, when John says:

   The good thing about Evelyn – and she has her good side, although she is most careful to hide it from strangers – is that she has absolutely no sense of humour. Which is very useful since it means you never have to waste your time trying to cheer her up. Because she's permanently unhappy. Misery is her natural state.

   page 61

- **Farce**: exaggerated actions and characteristics to give an absurd effect.
   For example, the actions of all the characters just at the point Colin enters (pages 25–9).

- **The running gag**: using something amusing over and over again. For example, knowing John relies on getting bargains leads to this dialogue:

   EVELYN   Nothing you ever get for us is quite right. I've got a vacuum cleaner with elastic bands holding on the attachments because you got them cheap off another model.

   JOHN   Oh, come on.

   EVELYN   I've got an electric mixer I can't use because it flings the food halfway up the bloody wall.

   JOHN   It's only because it's got the wrong bowl that's all. Only the bowl's wrong.

   EVELYN   Then why haven't we got the right bowl?

   JOHN   I'm trying to get hold of one. They're scarce.

   EVELYN   But it never did have the right bowl.

JOHN I know it didn't. How do you think I got it cheap in the first place?

page 20

- **Irony**: when one character thinks one thing when other characters and/or the audience know the opposite is true.
  For example, Colin says 'I'm glad I came round this afternoon. I don't know how you lot ever managed without me, eh?' (page 60). The irony is that his visit has caused greater chaos and destruction than he could possibly imagine.

- **Embarrassment**: when characters' actions are seen as embarrassing to an audience because of what the effects might be.
  For example, when Colin goes out to get the photographs of Carol, the other characters think they have offended him (pages 36–7).

- **Language**: careful use of language based on the characters and the situation can provide humour. For example, here it helps to create a comedy of manners:

  DIANA (*tense and shrill*) John, will you please sit down before you drive me mad.
  JOHN (*sitting*) Sorry. Sorry ...
  DIANA I'm sorry.
  JOHN No, it's me, I'm sorry.
  DIANA I'm sorry, John.
  JOHN No need to be sorry. That's all right.

page 22

- **Visual humour**: when actions rather than words make the audience laugh.
  For example, when Diana pours cream over Paul's head (page 52).

- **Verbal humour**: exchanges of words, one-liners, quips and jokes between the characters.
  For example, many of Evelyn's comments, or when John says: 'You must come to our house next time. Absolute

peace. Neither of us ever says a word to each other' (page 61).

Write down each of the above headings. Working in a group, go through the play noting down as many examples as you can find of each technique.

Now compare your lists. Are there any lines or incidents that occur under more than one heading? Discuss why that might be.

3 Using the notes you have gathered for Assignment 2 above, what statements can you devise to sum up the comic style of Alan Ayckbourn? Write an extended essay on this subject, using quotations and references from **Absent Friends** to support your argument.

4 Alan Ayckbourn uses language in different ways for his different characters. Look at this list of the various uses of language in the play:

- **Cliché**:   the use of a well-worn saying.
  For example '... it just doesn't cut any ice at all' (page 14).

- **Repetition and question**:   saying the same thing over and over again, sometimes to cover nervousness or to make a point. For example, when John says:

    No, the point I'm saying is, that if I were to knock off five per cent and sell the stuff to him for that much less, we could still net a profit of not less than what? – five twenties are a hundred – five eights are forty – less what? – three fives are fifteen – a hundred and twenty five per cent. That's an initial outlay – including transport, of what? – four nines are thirty-six – plus, say, twenty for handling either end – that's fifty-six. Bring it to a round figure – sixty ...

    page 34

- **Innuendo**:   suggesting something by the use of a word or the tone of voice. For example:

JOHN   Where's Paul?
MARGE Upstairs.
JOHN   Oh, both gone to bed, have they? (*He laughs*)

page 19

- **The weasel word and the filler**:   a weasel word (such as basically, really, certainly) is an empty word which is used to fill up thoughts but does not help the content of a sentence. Its name derives from the actions of a weasel which sucks the contents of an egg to leave it dry without substance. Fillers give people time to think (like, sort of, in fact and so on!). For example, when Diana is speaking to Evelyn at the beginning of the play:

  I mean, I know now I'm running myself down but Paul basically, he's got much more go – well, I mean let's face it, he's much cleverer than me. Let's face it. Basically. I mean, I was the bright one …

page 2

- **Sarcasm**:   like irony, something which is not necessarily true but in this case the tone of delivery is important.
  For example, when Colin talks about the day out they had some years before, he tells Evelyn: 'You missed something there, Evelyn.' Evelyn's reply is full of sarcasm: 'Sounds like it' (page 48).

Note down examples from the play of these different uses of language. You may already have found some in your search for Ayckbourn's comic devices (see pages 77–9). Using your notes, write an essay on the dramatic effects of language in **Absent Friends**.

Remember also that the *tone* can be just as important and effective – as when Evelyn reads out from a magazine twelve tips to keep the man in your life happy and then ends by saying: 'I'm not doing that for my bloody husband. He can stuff it' (page 12).

In performance

1. Imagine you are going to direct **Absent Friends**.
   Prepare a talk to your actors in which you include the following details:

   - how you think each character should be interpreted and played;
   - which parts of the play you feel are the most serious;
   - how you want some of the comedy played.

   You can choose any actors you want to play the parts – so feel free to direct your talk to any film, stage or television actors you might want. Money is no object!

2. Look at Diana's speeches:

   - pages 2–3 ('No, there are times when … some feeling for me.')
   - page 11 ('We knew him very well … need his friends.')
   - pages 55–6 ('When I was a little girl … I looked terrible.')
   - page 56 ('People used to say … I want to join the Mounted Police.')

   In pairs, decide how you think the part should be played. Insert stage directions (eye contact, gestures, body language etc.) and explain the tone and manner in which an actress should say these lines. Remember to have these in keeping with Diana's character from the rest of the play.

   When you have done this, act out the speeches.

3. Choose any section of the play you particularly enjoy to act out in a group. Three or four pages would be quite a good length – depending on what is happening dramatically. One of you could be the director and work on stage movements, gestures, body language and so on. Look at the stage set at the beginning of

Act One and decide how the characters should move, speak and react.

Remember there is always room for interpretation. A character could be played slightly differently depending on the actor, but it is essential to be faithful to the text.

When you have tried this, change the actors around to play different characters.

4 Read these extracts from reviews of different productions of **Absent Friends**.

- **Absent Friends** *is a serious, almost clinical, presentation of the nature of marriage where the most painful moments occur, not when the participants recognise its weaknesses, but when the outsider mistakes them for strengths. Peter Bowles [Paul] and Pat Heyward [Diana] play the lines with a perfect ear for all the undertones, a couple chained together by mutual weaknesses.*

  Alan Brien, **Plays and Players**, September 1975

- *Peter James's production confirms that it [**Absent Friends**] is one of the most discomforting of his [Ayckbourn's] bleak yet comic case-studies of modern marriages ... Disillusion is as much in the suburban air as Di's aerosol freshener. What pushes her and Paul's marriage to disaster is the arrival of Colin, who knew them when they were young and hopeful. His relentless belief in their fineness of character is undermining enough. But he is mourning a 'perfect woman', the fiancée he recently lost in a drowning accident. That means he can destroy the last remnants of their self-esteem by congratulating them on their luck in still having each other, and, inhibited as they are by respect for his grief, they can do nothing to stop him. It is a brilliant dramatic device.*

  Benedict Nightingale, **The Times**, 3 August 1992

- *The part of Colin is a masterly Ayckbourn creation. He is such a profoundly awful person, trite, platitudinous, and tirelessly cheerful, that I wondered ... whether his fiancée's accidental death was in fact suicide.*

Gary Bond plays him with bespectacled verve, totally oblivious to the hornets' nest he is stirring up with his relentless good nature. Instead of the sterile cul-de-sac in which his friends' relationships are so obviously stuck, he sees only happy marriages of pure love. Gesturing like some deeply sincere and over-active marsupial, he jumps up and down, chivvying the group into a reunion mood, telling stories about the good old days which (unwittingly) reveal past misdemeanours and cruelties.

Robert Gore-Langton, **The Daily Telegraph**, 3 August 1992

Write your own review of the play – from the text only if you have not had the opportunity of seeing the play live on the stage or in a television production.

Your review should contain a balance of:

- a summary of the main action
- comments on the themes
- personal opinion
- views on the performance, staging and directing.

5 Use a phrase or a sentence from one of the reviews as a springboard for an essay on the play. For example: 'How far do you agree that **Absent Friends** is a serious, almost clinical presentation of the nature of marriage?'

Use notes gathered in previous assignments to help you.

Extra scenes

1 In Act Two of **Absent Friends**, the characters discuss a day out at the Stately Home (pages 47–8).

Write the scene for this day out. Remember to look carefully at who was there and what happened. Think about how the characters would talk and act from information you have gained by reading the play (e.g. Colin's cheerfulness, John's nervousness etc.).

2 After the tea party Marge goes home to Gordon and tells him about the events of the afternoon. Write the conversation between Marge and Gordon.

Think about their characters and how Marge would describe, for example, Diana's outburst, Evelyn's confession of adultery, Colin's actions. To help with the conversation you write, remember what has happened to Gordon while Marge has been with the others.

3 Colin writes to Carol's parents to tell them about the tea party given in his honour. Write that letter. Remember he will have his own perspective on the events of the afternoon. Make sure the style is appropriate and in keeping with Colin's character as presented throughout the play.

4 Write the next act to the play. You can set it immediately after Colin leaves or some time afterwards. Include whichever characters you feel would be appropriate. Think about style, language, situation and character.

Study questions

Many of the activities you have already completed will help you to answer the following questions. Before you begin to write, consider these points about essay writing:

- Analyse what the question is asking. Do this by circling key words or phrases in red ink and numbering each part.

- Use each part of the question to 'brainstorm' ideas and references to the play which you think are relevant to the answer.

- Decide on the order in which you are going to tackle the parts of the question. It may help you to draw a flow-diagram of the parts so that you can see which aspects of the question are linked.

- Organise your ideas and quotations into sections to fit your flow-diagram. You can do this by placing notes in columns under the various headings.

- Write a first draft of your essay. Do not concern yourself too much with paragraphing and so on; just aim to get your ideas down on paper and do not be too critical of what you write.
- Redraft as many times as you need, ensuring all the time that:
  - each paragraph addresses the question;
  - each paragraph addresses a new part of the question, or at least develops a part;
  - you have an opening and closing paragraph which are clear and linked to the question set;
  - you have checked for spelling and other grammatical errors.

1. Choose two characters from **Absent Friends** and explain how they appear to be stereotypes at first but develop into more complex characters.

2. Why is Colin's innocence so important to the understanding of his character?

3. How does the language used by different characters make much of **Absent Friends** funny?

4. 'I don't know if you've ever met a perfect person. But that's what she was.' How *imperfect* are the characters in the play **Absent Friends** shown to be?

5. Discuss the main comic devices used in **Absent Friends**.

6. Alan Ayckbourn once described **Absent Friends** as 'claustrophobic, almost oppressive'. How far would you agree with his comments?

7. Choose four moments in the play which seem to combine humorous and serious sides to life and discuss how Alan

Ayckbourn manages to manipulate the reactions of his audience.

8 How far would you agree that Alan Ayckbourn presents a depressing view of marriage in the play *Absent Friends*?

9 Explain to someone who does not know the play *Absent Friends* how Alan Ayckbourn makes his audience laugh and cry.

10 Defend *Absent Friends* against a critic who claims that 'nothing happens' in the play.

Suggestions for further reading and comparing texts

Other plays by Alan Ayckbourn

Absurd Person Singular
First performed in 1972, about three couples who meet on three consecutive Christmas Eves at each others' homes. It combines very funny farcical action with much darker comedy, and looks at the state of marriage and strong and weak relationships.

The Norman Conquests
A trilogy first performed in 1973 – the most hilarious and clever example of plays revealing offstage, simultaneous and chronological action. The three plays (*Table Manners*, *Living Together*, and *Round and Round the Garden*) cover the action of a family weekend from 5.30 pm on a Saturday to 9 am on Monday from three perspectives – the dining room, the living room and the garden. Each play can be read or watched independently but when all three are seen, the audience can see exactly what happens to the characters when they are offstage in one of the other plays.

Bedroom Farce
First performed in 1975, one of Ayckbourn's innovations of three bedrooms simultaneously on show for the whole play with the action moving from one couple's bedroom to another as characters are followed visiting the occupants.

Sisterly Feelings
First performed in 1979, another theatrical frontier broken in a play about a family gathering after a funeral. At the end of each act a coin is tossed to decide which action should follow. Whether one character goes off with another, or whether the following act takes place in one venue or another, becomes totally dependent on how the coin lands. Interesting for the actors!

Invisible Friends
First performed in 1989, about a teenager, Lucy, whose imaginary friend, Zara, comes to life. She brings into Lucy's life a 'perfect' family to compensate for Lucy's real family who always appear to be rowing or moaning. Perfection, however, becomes for Lucy a real nightmare.

Plays by other writers

Blithe Spirit by Noël Coward
Written in 1941, this witty, delightfully dated 'English' play is concerned with the theme of death but deals with it in a very humorous way. The main character finds the mischievous spirit of his dead wife comes to visit at home where he and his present wife appear to be enjoying their life together.

She Stoops to Conquer by Oliver Goldsmith
Written in 1773, this is a wonderful example of the comic tradition involving all elements of farce, situation comedy, mistaken identities and great wit.

Abigail's Party by Mike Leigh
Like **Absent Friends**, this play takes place over a short period of time when a small group of friends gather to spend some time at

one person's home, while the daughter of one of them has a party just down the road. It has the same mix of serious and comic with carefully observed characters and a very dramatic ending.

Truly, Madly, Deeply by Anthony Minghella
Originally a film in which a dead man 'returns' to his grieving lover, this is a mixture of poignancy, humour, embarrassment and sheer delight.

The Importance of Being Earnest by Oscar Wilde
Written in 1895, a dazzling, witty comedy about society, manners and marriage with a wonderful 'tea' scene in Act Two.

Wider reading assignments

1. Write an extended essay on the use of different theatrical settings and techniques in two of Alan Ayckbourn's plays.

2. Write a comparative study of themes and ideas contained in **Absent Friends** and Mike Leigh's **Abigail's Party**.

3. Read **She Stoops to Conquer** or **The Importance of Being Earnest**. Discuss the similarities of the comic techniques used by one of these playwrights with Alan Ayckbourn's.

4. Michael Billington writes:

> *The truth is that most writers, dramatists certainly, harbour prejudices, preoccupations, areas of life that they make particularly their own: what is important is how dexterously they manage to find new ways of expressing their abiding concerns.*
> **Macmillan Modern Dramatists: Alan Ayckbourn**

In your own reading, how have writers managed to convey at the same time both the tragic and the comic in life?

5 Think about writers who have used the ritual of a tea party or a meal which has gone disastrously wrong. Examine common approaches and themes.

Pearson Education Limited
Edinburgh Gate, Harlow,
Essex, CM20 2JE, England
and Associated companies throughout the World.

First published in Great Britain by Chatto and Windus 1977
Copyright © Alan Ayckbourn 1977

Editorial material © Addison Wesley Longman 1966

This educational edition first published 1996
Tenth impression 2004

Editorial material set in 12/14 point Gill Sans
Printed in Malaysia, (GPS)

ISBN 0 582 30242 0

Acknowledgement

We are grateful to Plays and Players for permission to reproduce extracts
from their September 1975 issue.

Cover illustration by Paul Leith

The publisher's policy is to use paper manufactured from
sustainable forests.

Consultant: Geoff Barton